THE
Wisdom
of Trees

THE
Wisdom
of Trees

MYSTERIES, MAGIC, AND MEDICINE

text and photographs by Jane Gifford

Sterling Publishing Co., Inc.
New York

Library of Congress Cataloging-in-Publication
Data Available

10 9 8 7 6 5 4 3 2 1

Published in 2001 by
Sterling Publishing Company, Inc.
387 Park Avenue South, New York, N.Y. 10016
© 2000 Godsfield Press
Text © 2000 Jane Gifford

Distributed in Canada by Sterling Publishing
c/o Canadian Manda Group, One Atlantic Avenue,
Suite 105, Toronto,
Ontario, Canada M6K 3E7
Distributed in Australia by Capricorn Link (Australia)
Pty Ltd, P O. Box 6651, Baulkham Hills, Business
Centre, NSW 2153, Australia

Printed and bound in China

Sterling ISBN 0-8069-2786-0

Contents

The Celtic Wisdom of Trees

Mysteries, magic, and medicine

There is much that we in the modern world can learn from our tribal ancestors. Their understanding of the beneficial properties of the natural world was vast. Where ancient peoples have survived, along with the prehistoric landscapes which nurtured them, we are anxious to preserve this exotic knowledge and to learn from it.

ALTHOUGH INTEREST TODAY has largely been rekindled by the devastating rate at which these peoples and pockets of living history are being destroyed, it is thankfully revealing much ancient wisdom that has previously been unappreciated.

Trees have always been of paramount importance. Their benign value is not restricted to the Celtic world. We know, for example, that the trees of the tropical rainforest yield valuable medicines familiar for thousands of years to the indigenous peoples for whom the forest remains their home. Many of their uses are doubtless as yet undiscovered by modern science. Yet strangely we do not seem to value our own inherited wisdom in the same way. This book celebrates the enormous cultural and medicinal value of the trees most familiar in modern-day Europe from the point of view of our Celtic ancestors.

When the Romans invaded Great Britain nearly 2,000 years ago in 43 CE, they found a land peopled by individual tribes who were collectively known as the Celts. Although the Celts had no central government nor overall

leader, they shared many common beliefs. Ancestral reverence and a firm belief in the afterlife formed the foundation of their spirituality. They lived in harmony with the natural world and believed that the spirit behind creation was in all things, and that all things in nature had something valuable to teach humankind.

Great Britain then was largely a land of trees. Each species of tree had its own particular treasures to offer in terms of shelter, energy, food, and medicine. The well-being of the tribal peoples depended on the well-being of nature, and since trees had so much to offer, they were held in very high esteem.

The Celts had a vast storehouse of knowledge about the human relationship with the natural world. Specially trained elders, both men and women, committed the history and knowledge of their tribe to memory and passed it down in verse form through the generations. They were master poets and magicians who commanded enormous respect among their peoples. Poetry was then the most revered, and indeed feared, of all the creative arts. Training to be a poet was a long and complex process and took a minimum of twelve years to complete.

In Ireland these master poets were known as Ollaves and in Wales they were called Druids, a name now generally used to describe all such masters of the ways of our ancient ancestors. Symbolism and association were the keys to the wisdom of the Druids but since theirs was largely an oral tradition, unlocking the door to their secrets has always proved difficult. With no written records to leave behind and 2,000 years of religious persecution to contend with, very little remains of their perception and understanding of the natural world. The Celtic world view was outlawed in Britain and mainland Europe in the wake of Roman domination. It survived intact only in the memories of the learned ones and in the actions of those who persisted in the Old Ways. Because all of Ireland, the Isle of Man, and the remotest parts of Scotland, Wales, Cornwall, and Brittany escaped Roman influence for so much longer than the rest of Europe, the ways of the ancients have been best preserved in these places.

THE OGHAM

There was in fact a secret form of written language known only to the Druid initiates. This was called ogham. The letters of the ogham alphabet were cut as a series of notches on a piece of wood or stone in the form of strokes on either side of a straight line or stem. Some 360 stones with ogham inscriptions have been found in Great Britain and Ireland.

In the earliest-known form of ogham, the Tree Ogham or Celtic Tree Alphabet, each letter was associated with the name of a tree – the first letter, B, was given to Beth, the birch tree; the second letter, L, to Luis, the rowan tree, the third N, to Nion, which is the ash, and so on. The tradition lives on in Ireland today, where some of the names of the letters in the modern Irish alphabet are still the names of trees.

In an attempt to give this book some degree of organization and coherence, I have followed the Celtic tree alphabet and its associated tree calendar. The basic Celtic tree alphabet had twenty letters – fifteen consonants and five vowels with numerous additions to accommodate foreign language sounds. The Celtic year had thirteen months and each month was associated with a particular tree. Each of the letters in the alphabet had a wealth of symbolic wisdom behind it.

To the Druids, ogham was not only a way of communicating in secret. It was also one of the keys said to open the door to the spirit world. By understanding the mythology and associations behind each tree in the alphabet, the Druids could cross over into the Otherworld in order to bring back knowledge that would benefit the tribe. During their twelve years of intensive training, the Druids were expected not only to memorize the history and wisdom of the Celtic peoples but also some 150 forms of the ogham alphabet, such as the Colour Ogham and the Bird Ogham. Using these secret cipher languages Druids were able to have an apparently normal conversation in front of others while secretly saying something completely different. An understanding of ogham was a prerequisite for the membership of certain fellowships of knights and warriors, such as the Fianna, followers of the great Irish hero, Fionn mac Cumhaill (Finn MacColl).

The little that remains to us of ogham carved in stone is extremely difficult to decipher. Collections of Celtic mythology, like the 13th-century Red Book of Hergest or the Romances of medieval Brittany, give us some clues, but these records have often been later revised to suit the mood of the times or even deliberately jumbled to confuse all but the most learned Celtic scholars and poets. Even among academics there is little concurrence on how to write or to pronounce old Gaelic, let alone how to translate it.

As we have little understanding of this ancient tongue this book relies solely on the experts for guidance, trying to find some common thread among all their disagreements. Five hundred years of study has revealed some of the secrets hidden in the extant ogham inscriptions, but with so many types of ogham and so many systems of associated beliefs going back to the most ancient of times, it is hardly surprising that there is no consensus among academics as to their true meaning. But this is, of course, all part of the magic of ogham.

Ogham is said by the Irish to have been invented by Ogma Sunface, who was the god of eloquence of the ancient Celtic tribe, the Tuatha De Danaan (the People of Danu). This tribe is believed to have been a magical god-like race who arrived in Ireland in the 15th century BCE. The ancient goddesses of Ireland were called Banbha, Fodla, and Eire, three aspects of the White Goddess, the oldest and most powerful of all the ancient pantheon who has been present in her many guises throughout all time. That the Tree Ogham existed is beyond dispute, although the exact order in which the trees appeared in either the alphabet or the calendar is not. Although we can be sure of the individual letters used, their symbolic meanings remain obscure – just as the Druids intended – for only those in true possession of "the knowledge" were ever intended to comprehend the mysteries of the ogham.

This book follows, with a few exceptions, the order of the alphabet and calendar given by Robert Graves in his much disputed masterpiece *The White Goddess*, first published in 1946. However, every reader will have his or her own individual associations with trees and their seasons, and these will be as meaningful to them as any other interpretation. By losing yourself in the words and photographs in this book, your own personal relationship with Celtic tree magic will emerge. By piecing together the traditional uses and meanings given for each type of tree, you will begin to understand the vital nature of each tree's contribution to humankind and the ecosystem.

The Ogham Alphabet

The Celtic Tree Calendar

B — FOR BETH — *Birch*
DECEMBER 24th — JANUARY 20th

L — FOR LUIS — *Rowan*
JANUARY 21st — FEBRUARY 17th

N — FOR NION — *Ash*
FEBRUARY 18th — MARCH 17th

O — FOR ONN — *Gorse*
SPRING EQUINOX

F — FOR FEARN — *Alder*
MARCH 18th — APRIL 14th

S — FOR SAILLE — *Willow*
APRIL 15th — MAY 12th

H — FOR HUATH — *Hawthorn*
MAY 13th — JUNE 9th

D — FOR DUIR — *Oak*
JUNE 10th — JULY 17th

U — FOR URA — *Heather*
SUMMER SOLSTICE

T — FOR TINNE — *Holly*
JULY 18th — AUGUST 4th

C — FOR COLL — *Hazel*
AUGUST 5th — SEPTEMBER 1st

Q — FOR QUERT — *Apple*
SEPTEMBER 2nd — SEPTEMBER 29th

E — FOR EADHA — *Aspen*
AUTUMN EQUINOX

G — FOR GORT — *Ivy*
SEPTEMBER 30th — OCTOBER 27th

Ng — FOR NGETAL — *Broom*
OCTOBER 28th — NOVEMBER 24th

Ss — FOR STRAIF — *Blackthorn*
HALLOWE'EN (SAMHAIN)

R — FOR RUIS — *Elder*
NOVEMBER 25th — DECEMBER 21st

I — FOR IDHO — *Yew*
WINTER SOLSTICE

A — FOR ALIM — *Pine*
DECEMBER 23rd

Ph — FOR PHAGOS — *Beech*
THE WHOLE YEAR ROUND

Birch *The Lady of the Woods*

Beth

1st consonant of the Ogham Alphabet

DECEMBER 24TH – JANUARY 20TH

1st month of the Celtic Tree Calendar

ORIGIN OF THE NAME *MacBeth*

Emblem of Estonia and the Buchanan Clan

Betula pendula
SILVER BIRCH

Betula pubescens
DOWNY BIRCH

After the winter solstice as the days begin to lengthen again...

THE BIRCH WAS THE first tree to colonize Europe and North America after the last Ice Age some 13,000 years ago, so it is fitting that it should be the first consonant of the Tree Alphabet. The birch remains as much at home in the northern hemisphere today as it did in the past and there are 60 species still to be found. Despite its very delicate appearance, the birch is a pioneer tree which will find a foothold where most other trees will not grow. It is one of the main trees that is able to grow in inhospitable regions of the Arctic tundra and also in the ancient wild wood to be found in the highlands of Scotland, Ireland, and Wales.

The birch is fast-growing and acts as a nurse tree by offering protection to slower-growing trees like oak and pine which follow in its wake. It is easily recognized by the tracery of its delicate twigs and branches. Because its leaves are small and cast a light shadow other plants are easily able to grow in its shelter and this in turn encourages insects, birds and animals into the woods. Ironically, as more tender trees flourish under the protective birch, they often over-reach and smother the tree that has helped them.

Birch leaves are light and easily carried by the wind. They also rot easily, bringing nutrition to the earth and allowing other plants to establish themselves where they might not otherwise have been able to grow. A single birch produces millions of tiny seeds held in pendulous catkins, which dangle in the wind, allowing the seeds to be dispersed far and wide. Its timber is white, tough, and straight-grained with the unusual trait of showing no difference between the inner heartwood and the outer sapwood.

Relatively short-lived, the birch seldom lives longer than 80 years, going through youth, maturity, and senility in much the same time as we do. When young, its twigs are supple and bendy, growing harder and more brittle as the tree itself grows older. The trunk of the Silver Birch sheds its bark in papery strips and when the tree dies, the bark often remains standing as a delicate hollow tube, long after the inner wood has died and rotted away.

Fertile and prolific, graceful and nurturing, the Silver Birch was seen by our ancestors as the embodiment of the feminine principle. Wherever it had its stronghold it was the mainstay of human settlement.

Despite its delicate appearance, the birch is a pioneer tree, which will find a foothold where most other trees will not grow.

MYSTICAL ASSOCIATIONS

The first ogham inscription made in Ireland is said to have been written on a switch of birch. For the Celts, the birch was the Tree of Inception – the tree of new beginnings, birth and springtime, and a symbol of young love. In Pembrokeshire, Wales, a girl would give her sweetheart a piece of birch as a love token. The gift was a sign of encouragement meaning "you may begin." Associated with the pioneer spirit, birch implies the breaking of new ground and survival under extreme circumstances. As a bringer of strength and protection in adversity, the tree nurtures new life and its wood is believed to help ward off evil. Because of these associations babies' cradles are traditionally made from birch wood, and carrying a birch talisman is likewise said to protect you from any harm. Birch rods were used until very recently in the Isle of Man for flogging delinquents, in the belief that this would drive out the spirits that had apparently possessed them and caused their disruptive behavior.

The birch tree plays an important part in many of the year's oldest celebrations. Stripped of bark, it is the traditional Yule log that was burned during the midwinter ceremonies to drive out the spirit of the old year while welcoming in the new. The Old English Yule festival falls at the same time as the later Christian celebrations of the birth of Christ. A birch trunk is also traditionally used as the maypole because of its associations with fertility, birth, and springtime. The birch is the tree most associated with the

youthful aspect of the White Goddess, in particular in her role as bringer and protector of new life. The Triple Goddess appears in cultures throughout the world in three guises, as maiden, mother, and crone. The white bark of the Silver Birch is the goddess's mark and this color is also said to denote close links with the farie realms. For the Welsh Celts it is the tree of Arianrhod, who

The birch is the tree of new beginnings, of birth and springtime, and a symbol of young love.

is in charge of the Silver Wheel of the Heavens and who presides over birth and initiation, and of the virginal goddess Blodeuwedd, who was created from nine types of flower as a consort for the Welsh sky god, Llew. The Anglo-Saxons used the birch tree to evoke Eostre, goddess of fertility and springtime. For Nordic peoples, the birch was the tree of Frigga, goddess of married love, and of Freya, Norse goddess of love and fecundity. The Babylonians called her Ishtar and the ancient Egyptians, Isis. In Teutonic mythology, the Last Battle of the World will be fought around a birch tree.

The birch is the Cosmic Tree of Celtic shamanism. Druids visualized its white trunk when climbing up through the different planetary spheres to communicate with the

World Spirit. Importantly it is also beside the birch that the hallucinogenic and potentially very toxic toadstool Fly Agaric (*Amanita muscaria*) is most often found.

Thought to be soma, the divine mushroom of immortality of the ancient Etruscans, Fly Agaric was used by the Celtic shaman as an aid to Otherworld journeying. Its use can, however, prove fatal and it should never be experimented with. The birch itself has many healing properties, particularly related to rheumatism and arthritis, common ailments in the northern lands where the tree has its stronghold. It is also useful for purging the system and for skin complaints. For the ancient Celts, the whiteness of the tree's bark was a sign of its purifying nature.

LESSON OF THE BIRCH

The birch tree symbolizes a fresh start and can bring courage and determination to those of us who are treading the path of spiritual growth and development for the first time. Although the birch does appear fragile, it is in fact extremely hardy. This teaches us that in apparent weakness there is often to be found great strength. The birch also promises new life and love, and is a potent symbol of purification and renewal, which focuses our attention on our potential for change and on the consideration of new directions and goals to be experienced in our lives. It teaches the lesson of unselfishness and of caring for the needs of others in ways that help them to flourish of their own accord.

The birch has many healing properties – especially related to rheumatism and arthritis.

Fly agaric toadstools are most often found under birch trees.

HEALING

Oil from birch *bark* can be used for treating skin conditions such as eczema. It also makes a good insect repellent. The *buds* make a refreshing tonic for use in hair preparations and the *sap* is a natural shampoo. North American Indians make a syrup from the sap of the *Cherry Birch* as a remedy for dysentery as well as genito-urinary infections. Birch sap is also widely used to make tonic wine and a tonic tea is made using birch *bark* and wintergreen, which are two of the main flavorings used in the popular American drink, root beer. An infusion made from birch *leaves* is antiseptic and a diuretic. It was recommended by Culpeper, the 17th-century herbalist and physician, for breaking down gall and kidney stones and as a mouthwash. The *buds*, *leaves*, and *bark* are used in traditional remedies for rheumatism, arthritis, and urinary tract infections such as cystitis. The *essential oil* is used today to treat all of these ailments and also cellulitis, muscle pain, obesity, and oedema. In vibrational medicine, *Essence of Birch* is useful for those who find it difficult to express themselves. Associated with beauty and calmness, its vibration heightens tolerance of one-self and others.

The *young leaves* can be collected in late spring and early summer. To make an infusion, put 1 or 2 teaspoons of fresh or dried leaves in a cup and steep in boiling water. Leave to infuse for 10 minutes. Strain and sweeten with honey if desired. Drink 3 times a day. An inhalation made from a handful of *fresh leaves* in a bowl of boiling water will help clear a blocked nose, ease sinuses, and shift catarrh.

Collect bark in late summer. Never cut the bark off all the way round the trunk as this will kill the tree. It is best to take only a little bark from each tree. Apply freshly cut bark with the internal wet side against the skin to help ease muscle pain.

Collect the sap in early spring by drilling a 7cm hole at a 45 degree angle into the trunk. Never take more than a pint from a single tree and plug the hole carefully afterward as the sap will continue to bleed from the trunk and weaken the tree.

Color White   *Planet* Venus

Stone Crystal   *Polarity* Feminine

Elements Air, Water

Deities Arianrhod, Blodeuwedd, Frigga, Freya, Eostre

Inception

Purity + Cleanliness

Love + Friendship

Birth + Initiation

Rowan *The Lady of the Mountains*

Luis
2nd consonant of the Ogham Alphabet

Sorbus aucuparia
ROWAN

As the sap begins to rise...

THERE ARE MORE than 100 species of mountain ash that are distributed throughout northern temperate regions of the world, as far afield as China, northern Europe, and North America. The species most familiar to the Celts would have been *Sorbus aucuparia*, the rowan. It is still a frequent and welcome sight on the mountains of Ireland, Scotland, and Wales, where the Celts had their last strongholds. Although the rowan flourishes in the company of other trees, it seldom forms a wood in its own right. A mature tree usually grows to around 30 feet (9 m), although it can grow to twice this height. Its lifespan is around 200 years.

The rowan is a slender tree with smooth, gray bark and elegant, upward-reaching branches. It is as happy growing on exposed mountain crags as it is on lowland heath and pasture. Rowan trees produce masses of creamy white flowers in May, which grow into dense clusters about the size of an adult hand. Each tiny flower has five petals and five sepals. The round fruits, green at first, ripen to a rich orange-red as fall progresses. Each rowan berry has a tiny five-pointed star – the pentogram, ancient symbol of magical protection – opposite its stalk. The tree has been widely planted by remote farms, in graveyards, and near stone circles for protection, and in gardens and along roadsides for its ornamental value. The number five is one of the numbers associated with the White Goddess and to the Celts this fivefold division marked the rowan as one of her sacred trees. In fall, the leaves of the rowan can change from green to shades of pink and gold. Sometimes the berries remain on the tree after the leaves have fallen, depending how hungry the birds have been. Although commonly called the mountain ash, the rowan is not a true ash: it is actually a member of the rose family.

The rowan tree's many names reveal its nature: Lady of the Mountains, Mountain Ash, Quickbeam, Quicken Tree, Witch.

MYSTICAL ASSOCIATIONS

The rowan is sacred to the English goddess Brigantia and to Brigid, ancient muse of the Irish Celts. From Brigid comes the divine inspiration behind poetry, music, and the arts. Rowan blossom announces the annual return of the young goddess to the spring mountainsides and, when birds fill the rowan's branches with song after feasting on its fall berries, it is easy to understand why the Celts associated the rowan with divine inspiration and the creative arts. One of the many poetic names the Celts had for rowan is "delight of the eye." The red and green contrast of the rowan tree's berries and leaves is thought to have been the inspiration behind the tartans of the Celtic clans.

Brigantia and Brigid are both aspects of the White Goddess in her role as protector of pastoral people and their livestock. Brigid is daughter of the Dagda, Lord and Guardian of Nature, one of the most revered of the Old Irish gods. Both goddesses are associated with the promise of spring and fertility, and both have fiery arrows of rowan wood that they shoot blazing through the seasons, following the arc of the sun through the year. As goddesses of spinning and weaving, they prepare the neverending fabric of life and guide the passage of the sun through the constellations and the cycle of the seasons. Rowan was thus the wood traditionally used for making spindles and spinning wheels.

The Celtic festival of Imbolc on February 1st is sacred to Brigid as she kindles the

The rowan is a
sacred and magical
tree – a symbol of
the hidden mysteries
of Nature and the
quickening of the
life force.

divine fire of inspirations and visions, and reawakens the spirit of the year. It is also the first of the four Cross-Quarter Days on which witches celebrate their Sabbaths. Brigid's festival has been incorporated into the Christian calendar as the Feast Day of Saint Brigid, which is also celebrated at the beginning of February. Saint Brigid tends the fire of faith and her caldron is filled with the milk of human kindness. The Roman festival of Candlemas also falls at this time. Candlemas is celebrated by the Christian Church as the Feast of the Purification of the Blessed Virgin Mary. More recently it has been renamed Lady Day, a term much more resonant of its ancient associations.

All parts of the rowan tree are said to promote spiritual and physical healing.

To the Celts, the rowan was a symbol of the hidden mysteries of nature and the quickening of the life force. A sacred and magical tree, rowan offered many kinds of protection against enchantment and illness, and it was considered most unlucky to fell one. The rowan was associated with visions and portents, with vitality and reawakening, and with spiritual strength. The rowan is intimately associated with serpents and dragons and the tree was believed to protect earth energies in ley lines and standing stones. The Druids often planted rowans at places of worship and they used the smoke from rowan fires to call up spirit guides and warriors. Rowan smoke was also traditionally used to foretell the future of lovers.

In Wales, rowan was planted in churchyards to protect the spirits of the dead, while carrying two rowan twigs tied into a cross with red ribbon was said to offer protection from the dead at Samhain (Hallowe'en). Boughs of rowan are still hung over stables and dairies in many parts of Britain to protect livestock from barrenness and harm. Rowan twigs, known as witch wands, are used for metal divining.

The rowan has a special place in many mythologies. In Scandinavian and Irish myth, the first woman was born from a rowan tree. In Greek legend, the rowan itself was born from the blood and feathers of an eagle, which fell to the ground as the divine bird battled with demons to save the cup from which the gods drank nectar. The rowan's red berries and feathery leaves are a mark of the sacred eagle's spirit. Yule legends say that a star shone on top of the rowan tree to herald the return of light and life to the world of darkness, just as a star was later said to have shone over the stable when Christ was born, to show where he was.

As well as warding off evil, carrying a rowan talisman is said to increase your psychic powers and improve your chances of success. Rowan berries and bark bring good luck and all parts of the tree are said to promote spiritual and physical healing. In the Irish Romance of Fraoth, the berries of the magical rowan were guarded by a dragon and contained the nourishment of nine meals. They could heal the wounded and add a year to a person's life. The Quickening Tree of Dubhous, another magical rowan, had marvelous berries that could transform a one-hundred-year-old man into a youthful thirty-year-old.

LESSON OF THE ROWAN

Rowan is able to flourish higher up on the mountains than most other trees. Closer to the sun and divine inspiration in this extreme environment, it yet retains its grace of form and its potential for healing. Exposed to the elements on solitary crags, it still produces blossom and berries to delight the eye and heal the body, bringing vibrant color and birdsong to the hills. Rowan emphasizes the need for color and creative endeavor in our lives and encourages us to open our minds to creative inspiration. It also teaches us that we can draw on the forces of life to heal ourselves and those around us. We can develop the art of turning adversity into creative opportunity. Rowan protects and gives courage and strength to those walking the path of spiritual growth and enlightenment. For the Celts, the rowan was the Tree of Quickening, of Sacred Fire, of the Awakening Spirit, and the Sun.

Growing high up on the side of mountains the rowan seems closer to the sun and the force of divine inspiration.

❧ HEALING ❧

From ancient legend it is clear that the healing powers of rowan have long been recognized and the *ripe berries* do indeed contain large amounts of organic acids, tannins, sugars, and Vitamin C. These make them mildly purgative and diuretic, and preparations made from them are a general tonic for the body. They are a traditional laxative and are used in the treatment of kidney disorders. The high concentration of Vitamin C in the fruit has made them a valuable preventive and cure for scurvy. The berries have been used for the commercial extraction of Vitamin C and also in the manufacture of "sorbose," a sweetener used in diabetic foods.

In vibrational medicine, *Essence of Rowan* attunes us to the energies of nature, broadening perspectives and allowing a deeper understanding of our place in the universe. In *meditation*, rowan helps clear the mind, opening us up to inspiration. The sight alone of a rowan tree decked with berries and full of birdsong can help heal the human spirit and lift the mood.

❧

Color Green *Planet* The Sun

Stone Tourmaline *Polarity* Feminine

Deities Brigantia, Brigid,

Virgin Mary

Quickening + Sacred Fire

Vitality + Spiritual Strength

Creative Inspiration

Ash *The World Tree; Tree of Life*

Nion
3rd consonant of the Ogham Alphabet

FEBRUARY 18TH – MARCH 17TH
3rd month of the Celtic Tree Calendar

Fraxinus excelsior
COMMON ASH

Month of floods...

THE COMMON ASH is native to northern Europe and the British Isles. It thrives on damp, lime-rich soils and is one of the main trees to be found in lowland woods. The ash is graceful, with pale gray bark and feathery leaves. Although smooth when young, the bark furrows with age, until eventually deep ridges run in ripples up the trunks of mature trees. Ash woods are light and airy and the trees grow quickly, although they tend to sour the soil around them, so other plants do not thrive there. The timber is strong and highly elastic and does not split when worked. Because the timber is extremely useful, ash woods were generally coppiced. This involved harvesting the wood by cutting the tree back to ground level every ten years or so, and allowing it to regrow. The natural lifespan of the ash is around 200 years but a single coppiced tree can live for 1,000 years or more. The ash can withstand storm-force winds because its roots grow deeply and spread for some distance around the tree, but it seems also to attract lightning, hence the expression "Avoid an ash, for it courts a flash."

The ash's branches grow upward, dipping down toward their ends but then rising once more so that their tips reach toward the sky. The buds of the ash are its most distinctive part. They are sooty black, covered in hairs, and have a phallic appearance. As the sap rises in spring, ash buds begin to ooze sticky resin. Strange petal-less flowers with purple stamens appear in April, long before the leaves unfurl. Flowers of both sexes, as well as hermaphrodite flowers, can all occur on the same tree, and while some ashes are predominantly male, others are predominantly female. The ash bears single winged seeds, known as keys, but it does not begin to produce fertile fruit until it is at least forty years old. The ash is one of the last trees to come into leaf in spring and it is often the first tree to lose its leaves in the fall. It has a special affinity with water and ash leaves have a triangular conduit running down their center stem, where tiny hairs absorb moisture as it trickles down the leaf.

There are more than sixty species of ash to be found throughout Europe, Asia, and North America and it is a member of the olive family. The leaves of the Common Ash almost always have an odd number of leaflets and to find an even number is considered as lucky as finding a four-leafed clover.

The ash is one of the last trees to come into leaf in the spring.

MYSTICAL ASSOCIATIONS

The ash is central to the beliefs of many ancient world cultures and is thought to be the tree from which the essence of humankind originated. The ash was always of great magical importance to the ancient Irish. In the early histories of Ireland, it is said that five magical trees protected the land; three of these were ash trees, the other two were yew and oak. The magical ash trees were called the Tree of Tortu, the Tree of Dathi, and the Branching Tree of Uisnech. The Irish ollaves are said to have felled these trees themselves in 665 CE, as a symbol of the destruction of paganism by Christianity. Saint Patrick began this process in the 5th century CE, when he is said to have driven all serpents out of Ireland with the aid of an ash stick. To the Celtic people, the serpent represented female earth energy and so to them this act of Saint Patrick's also symbolized the banishment of the goddess from involvement in the affairs of humankind.

In Northern European legend, the ash is seen as the Great World Tree, a symbol of universality, which spreads its roots and branches over every land and forms a link between the gods, humankind, and the dead.

The ash tree forms a link between the gods, humankind, and the dead in the spirit world.

Yggdrasill, the Enchanted Ash, marked the center of the universe, around which everything flowed. At its root was a serpent that represented female earth energies and in its crown was an eagle that was symbolic of the male energies of the sky. In ancient Scandinavian legend three goddesses known as the Three Norns dispensed justice from beneath the sacred ash.

The Greek goddess Nemesis also carried an ash branch as an instrument of divine justice on behalf of the gods. She punished through humiliation those who did not show sufficient gratitude for her bounty. She and the goddesses of many other cultures measured out mortal happiness and misery under the guardianship of the ash tree.

The Vikings believed that the first man was born of ash and their god, Odin, hung himself from this magical tree to receive illumination in the shape of the runes – an ancient form of writing similar to ogham – that contained the understanding of all the world. The Viking runes were recorded on tablets of ash and the Vikings themselves are said to have been known as *Aescling*, "Men of Ash," because of their great reliance on the magic of this tree. Viking culture was quickly assimilated in Ireland and the traditional Old Irish emphasis on the earth goddesses associated with the ash tree became focused rather more on the masculine principles of the power of the sky and of the sun gods.

The ash eventually replaced the birch as the maypole, becoming a symbol of the creative life-giving energy of the sun god, instead of being a celebration of the potential of the virgin goddess as it once was.

The ash is also connected to the waters of life and is associated with the sea. In ancient Wales and Ireland, water-loving ash was always used for coracle slats and oars, and sailors carried an equal-armed cross carved from ash wood to protect them at sea. The ash is sacred to Poseidon, whose palace is beneath the ocean.

To the Celts the enchanted ash was symbolic of Universal Order. It holds a key to Universal Truth.

Ash was considered one of the best woods for making spears and the possession of a staff of ash was said to protect against malign influences. A Druid's wand made from ash, found on Anglesey in North Wales, is thought to date from the early part of the 1st century CE. To the Druids, the ash holds a key to Universal Truth. It is the Tree of Balance and the Marriage of Opposites, and it links our inner and outer worlds. This bipolarity theme of balanced energies can be clearly seen in the physical properties of the ash tree. Ruled by the male energy of the sun, the ash still has a special relationship with the female element of water. The ash's form is one of feminine grace, yet its buds are brazenly phallic and its flowers can be both bisexual or of a single sex.

In perfect harmony, the ash's branches reach as far into the sky as its roots grow into the earth. To the Celts, this was all symbolic of Universal Order. Like the enchanted ash, they saw themselves as an integral part of the flow of the universe. They understood that every action and thought formed part of an endless chain of events and that each and every thing is an essential part of the whole. They believed that whatever was done in the physical world would affect all other levels of existence. The Druids represented these different levels of existence as the "Three Circles of Being" – Abred, Gwynedd, and Ceugant. These can be translated into endless trinities such as Past, Present, and Future; Physical, Mental, and Spiritual; Chaos,

Balance, and Creative Force. The Circles of Being are all interlinked so that whatever happens on one level will inevitably affect the other two. The Celts believed that for every action there is a reaction and that whatever we do inevitably affects everything else that might happen. We are all an important part of the Universal Order and there is no escaping the consequences of our human existence in the neverending cycle of life. For the Celts, the ash was the guardian of these universal truths.

Beechwood fires are bright and clear,
If the logs are kept a year.
Chestnut's only good, they say,
If for long it's laid away.
Make a fire of elder tree,
Death within your house shall be.
But ash new or ash old
Is fit for a queen with a
crown of gold.

Birch and fir logs burn too fast,
Blaze up bright and do not last.
It is by the Irish said,
Hawthorn bakes the sweetest bread.
Elm wood burns like
churchyard mold,
E'en the flames are cold.

But ash green or ash brown
Is fit for a queen with a
golden crown.

Poplar gives a bitter smoke,
Fills your eyes and makes you choke.
Applewood will scent your room
With an incense-like perfume.
Oaken logs if dry and old,
Keep away the winter's cold.
But ash new or ash old
Is fit for a queen with a
crown of gold.

ANON, FOUND IN THE PLOUGH INN,
MYDDFAI, DYFED, MAY 1998

LESSON OF THE ASH

Through their understanding of Universal Order and their appreciation of their own unique role in it, the Celts discovered a deep sense of belonging and a purpose for their existence. Our modern and hectic daily life is usually far removed from the cycles and forces of the natural world, and it can often seem empty of any real purpose. The ash is a key to healing the loneliness of the human spirit out of touch with its origins – it can provide a sense of being grounded and of belonging. The ash reminded the Celts of the interlinking of the Three Cycles of Being. Likewise we are encouraged to consider the role of the past in creating the present, so that we can better appreciate the many ways in which positive thought and action today can help to create a brighter tomorrow. Through a constant process of balancing and marrying opposites, we, like the ash, can achieve harmony within ourselves.

Ash is a key to healing the loneliness of the human spirit out of touch with its origins.

❧ HEALING ❧

In ancient Britain the ash was associated with rebirth and new life and was famous for its ability to heal children, who were passed through a split in the tree's trunk in order to be cured. The ash has some more conventional medicinal properties but its main potential for healing is in the realm of *meditation*. In modern kinesiology, *Essence of Ash* is associated with strength. It promotes harmony and a feeling of being "in tune" with your surroundings, and also gives strength and flexibility.

An infusion made from bitter ash *bark* is mildly laxative and diuretic. The bark from the *root* is considered most potent and in early medicine it was used for its tonic and astringent properties in treating liver diseases and arthritic rheumatism. Ash *bark* and *leaves* are used by herbalists today to regulate bowel movements, to expel intestinal parasites, to reduce fever, to treat kidney and urinary infections, and to alleviate rheumatic and gouty pains.

The *bark* of the ash has also been used as a substitute for quinine in the treatment of malaria.

Wearing garters of green ash bark was once believed to offer protection against the powers of magicians, while those who ate the buds of ash on Midsummer's Eve were said to become invulnerable to the influence of witches. The leaves were thought to attract love and prosperity, and sleeping with fresh leaves under your pillow is said to bring psychic dreams.

❧

Color White *Planets* The Sun and Neptune

Stone Turquoise *Polarity* Feminine

Elements Air, Water

Deities Odin, Nemesis, Poseidon, Neptune

Balance + Harmony

Universal Order

Power of Positive Thought

Sea Power

Golden Gorse

Onn

2nd vowel of the Ogham Alphabet

Sign of hope...

MARCH 21ST
Spring Equinox

OTHER NAMES *Furze, Whin*

Ulex europaeus
COMMON GORSE

Ulex gallii
WESTERN GORSE

Ulex minor
DWARF GORSE

"WHEN GORSE IS in bloom kissing is in season." There are many versions of this old country saying but the point of them all is that gorse is never really out of flower, so there will always be time for kissing. Whatever the time of year, if you look around the heaths, sea cliffs, and open hillsides where gorse is most often found, there will always be, somewhere, a golden-yellow gorse flower to brighten the day.

Although it prefers acid soils, gorse will find a foothold on rough grassland almost anywhere. It is a dense evergreen shrub with sharp spines for its smaller branches and twigs, which divide into even more sharp spines for its leaves. It has no normal flat leaves, except when young, and is a very resilient plant, able to survive in the wind and extreme cold, offering valuable shelter on exposed land: it is an excellent windbreak. Its spiny leaves reduce water loss, so whether baked by the sun or drenched in salt water, gorse is able to flower almost continuously and quickly colonizes open ground, growing up to around 7 feet (2.1 m) tall.

From early spring right through the summer, gorse flowers so generously that the plant itself is often lost under a deep mass of vibrant yellow blooms. They are strongly scented and, on a still day, the air is rich with the sweet fragrance of coconut and vanilla, intense and evocative. The hum of bees is interrupted by the crack of the gorse's seed pods as they explode in the heat of the sun, releasing thousands of tiny seeds. Gorse burns easily and fiercely and was a valuable fuel, especially since it grows in places where wood is often scarce. In early spring, while the ground is still damp, farmers light "furze fires" to burn off the old woody stems of the gorse and to encourage fresh young growth for livestock to graze on. Gorse reaches its peak of flowering in April, painting the landscape early with the color of golden sunshine and offering bees their first chance in the year to make honey.

Whatever the time of year, somewhere a golden yellow gorse can be found to brighten the day.

MYSTICAL ASSOCIATIONS

With their love of strong color, the ancient Celts no doubt welcomed the brilliant yellow tide that sweeps across the landscape when gorse comes into full flower in spring. Its intense golden-yellow flowers lift the spirits, attracting bees and holding the promise of honey to come. The gorse's golden flowers symbolized the energy of the sun and the sun god Lugh, Celtic god of light and genius, and honey was a symbol of wisdom acquired through hard work and dedication. By flowering all the year round and remaining evergreen, gorse carries within it a spark of the sun god's life-giving energy, through even the darkest months of winter. Gorse was a sign of encouragement and a promise of good things to come. It was pleasing to the senses and restored faith in the downhearted. The Feast of Lugh (August 1st), Lughnasa in the Celtic calendar, is known in Brittany as the Festival of the Golden Gorse. Gorse was particularly important to heath dwellers for whom it was often the only fuel. Bakers preferred gorse for their ovens because the wood is dry and burns hot. Gorse also provides good grazing, if burned back in spring, and, cut or growing, it quickly makes a windbreak or a fence. You can even use gorse to hang your washing on to dry. Impaled on the spines, laundry will stay safely in place, even in high winds. A decoction of the flowers is said to be good against jaundice and in Welsh folklore, gorse is said to give protection against witches.

LESSON OF THE GORSE

The flowering of the gorse provides a splash of color and inspiration, even on the darkest days, reminding us to remain positive and focused whatever life throws at us. Gorse brings hope to the disillusioned and brightens those who are despondent. Gorse thickets are spiny and may seem impenetrable but find a way to deal with them, and they can provide food and shelter for the mind and body, and fragrance to soothe the senses. The gorse carries the sun through every season and it teaches the importance of constancy, hope, and faith in times of disappointment. We need to take stock and restore faith in ourselves and in our dreams from time to time. Gorse promises that effort will be rewarded when we honor our achievements. For the Celts, gorse was symbolic of optimism and good faith.

> Gorse carries the sun through every season and teaches constancy, hope, and faith in times of disappointment.

❦ HEALING ❦

The *Bach Flower Remedy* made from gorse
is given to those who have given up hope
and who feel that they are beyond helping,
especially those who are faced with
a serious illness.

Greenman Essence of Gorse is used to ease
frustration, restlessness, and jealousy,
promoting emotional security and a feeling
of deep, inner joy.

❦

Color Yellow *Planet* The Sun

Stone Topaz *Polarity* Feminine

Deity Lugh (Llew in Wales)

Restoration of Faith

Hope + Optimism

Gathering of Strength

Alder *Tree of the God Bran*

Fearn
4th consonant of the Ogham Alphabet

MARCH 18TH – APRIL 14TH
4th month of the Celtic Tree Calendar

MARCH 21ST – *Spring Equinox*

Alnus glutinosa
COMMON ALDER

Alnus incana
EUROPEAN, OR
GRAY ALDER

Alnus cordata
ITALIAN ALDER

The drying of the winter floods...

THE ALDER IS A tree of the northern hemisphere. It is an ancient tree that has grown for millions of years and it is still a common sight along riverbanks, on boggy fens and marshes, and in wet woods throughout Europe. The alder is unusual as it is the only broad-leaved tree to produce cones and is especially easy to recognize in winter, when last year's cones, the present year's catkins, and the new leaf buds can all be seen on the same tree.

Alder catkins form in the year prior to their flowering, remaining dormant on the tree throughout winter and opening in spring before the leaves unfurl. Male catkins are pendulous with purple-red scales and yellow flowers whereas the female catkins, borne on the same tree as the males, are much smaller. After fertilization, the female catkins develop into tiny green cones, which age to become a dark brown color. It takes roughly thirty years before the alder tree is capable of producing a full crop of seeds.

> *"the lengthening month of the waking alder"*
> LENCT

The alder is a beneficial tree that enriches the soil around it by binding nitrogen salts in its root system. The tree is delicately proportioned, yet it has immense underlying strength: its timber resists decay even when submerged in water, hardening with time to the toughness of stone. With roots that enrich the soil and wood that withstands the erosive power of water, and which grows even stronger when submerged, the alder was already a special tree in the eyes of our ancient ancestors. Alder wood was also used for the making of walkways across otherwise impassable marshlands, and it was also an essential timber used for the construction of the ancient Celtic lake dwellings that were known as crannogs. These were raised above the water on deeply sunk piles of alder. But the water-loving alder was especially revered because it appeared to bleed when felled – the wood, which is white when first cut, slowly turns red when exposed to the air.

Alder roots enrich the soil. The timber hardens in water to the toughness of stone.

MYSTICAL ASSOCIATIONS

Alder's Celtic calendar month, from mid-March to mid-April, is the month of lengthening daylight and increasing bounty. It marks the drying up of the winter floods and the growing warmth of the sun. Just as the homes of the ancient Celts were raised above the floods on piles of alder, so were their spirits also lifted by the alder's early flowering and its many useful gifts. The alder was held as sacred for the sacrifice of its wood and for its beneficial effect on the soil, and the tree was symbolic of the generosity of the gods and the health of the land. The alder was a protective tree that was believed to enable access into the farie realms but it was also said that if you felled a sacred alder, your house would be burned to the ground. In Irish legend the first human male was created from alder, as the first female was made from rowan.

The alder has many associations with the more kindly and compassionate gods. It is the totem tree of the much-loved pagan god Bran, who was one of the guardians of ancient Britain. Bran is especially important to the Welsh. Legend tells how Bran, when close to death, gave his men instructions to cut off his head and to carry it to London, spending seven years in Harlech and eighty years in Pembroke on the way there. Bran's head remained alive and did not decay, and he continued to advise his followers through his songs. Bran's oracular head was buried in the White Hill beneath the Tower of

London. His shamanistic birds were ravens, which acted as his scouts and messengers. The raven became one of Britain's most important totem creatures and throughout Celtic history this bird was regarded as a guise of the White Goddess. With their sadly clipped wings, the present-day ravens at the Tower of London are a legacy of this legend. It is said that Britain will fall if they ever desert the Tower.

Bran was a generous and caring god who ruled his people well, just as alder is a beneficial tree, both to the land and to the life it supports. Indeed, Bran was so dear to the British people that the Christian Church sanctified him, so he became known as Saint Brons or Bran the Blessed. Cronos, god of ancient Greece, was also associated with the alder and with prophetic ravens, as were Apollo, Odin, the Celtic god Lugh, and King Arthur of the Britons. In Norse legends,

March was known as the lengthening month of the waking alder, a time known as Lenct. This was a period of enforced fasting as winter provisions ran low. This time of fasting was perhaps the origin of the Christian festival of Lent: the names are certainly similar.

Alder was also revered as the source of fine, strongly colored dyes, so much admired by the flamboyant Celts. The flowers provide the green dye associated with farie clothes. A fiery red dye is made from the bark and, if metal sulfates (known as copperas) are added, this turns black. The young shoots produce a cinnamon color, which, with copperas, goes pure yellow. Alder, like rowan, was therefore associated with the art of fabric-making and the goddesses of spinning like Arianrhod. The Celts believed that magical intent could be bound into a fabric during its making, so dyers, spinners, and weavers were greatly

Alder is the totem tree of the pagan god Bran, one of the guardians of ancient Britain.

respected for their art. The actual purple color of the alder's buds is associated with the god Bran and is called "royal purple."

Alder wood makes a poor fuel but excellent charcoal and its hot fire was prized among ancient Celtic metalworkers and smiths for forging ritual weapons. Once hardened, alder wood was also ideal for making warriors' shields. More recently, alder charcoal's main commercial use was in the making of gunpowder. In Ireland alder is the traditional wood for dairy vessels and English alder is the best wood for making clogs. Alder has a long tradition in the making of bridges, jetties, sluices, and pumps, as well as in providing the foundations of many buildings; 16th-century Venice is built on alder piles. Alder also proved the ideal timber for the making of lockgates.

LESSON OF THE ALDER

The alder is a tree that supports and protects physically, emotionally, and spiritually. Its associations with both weapons and shields reminded the ancient Celts that part of the skill of the warrior lies in knowing when to take up the sword and when to take up the shield. Although an alder shield will protect you and give you courage and an alder-forged weapon will help you defend yourself, ultimately the most important aspect of the warrior is his or her intent. This is the key to success or failure. The alder reminds us of the need to blend strength and courage with generosity of spirit and compassion. There is a time to challenge things and a time to hold our peace. The alder teaches us this discrimination and the need to see beneath the surface of things. It combines the desire for self-preservation with the desire to serve and emphasizes the need for a firm foundation to stand on.

The alder reminded our ancient ancestors of the need to blend strength and courage with generosity of spirit and compassion.

HEALING

The sticky *young leaves* and the *bark* of the alder are used medicinally. The constituents include tannins and anthraquinones, which give alder an astringent action and a bitter taste. Alder leaves and bark are used by herbalists to treat enteritis, severe diarrhoea, fever, colds, and rheumatic pain. A decoction of alder can also be used as a mouthwash and as a gargle to soothe tonsilitis. Alder has the ability to dissolve puffiness and swelling and a decoction of the leaves or bark is a traditional remedy for burns and inflammations. Culpeper recommended bathing in a *decoction of alder bark* to relieve the pain in such cases. In general alder bark gives much the same relief as alder leaves but, when fresh, the leaves also have several particular uses: when crushed, *freshly picked leaves* will soothe chapped skin and, if placed in the shoes, they will refresh tired feet. Alder leaves, collected with the dew on them, were once placed around houses to rid them of fleas, trapping the tiny pests in their sticky resin. Beds of *dried alder leaves* were anciently renowned for giving relief from rheumatism. In modern kinesiology, *Essence of Alder* is associated with the principle of release. It reduces stress, anxiety, and nervousness and increases life energy. Alder helps us to become strong.

Color Purple

Stone Amethyst *Polarity* Masculine

Elements Fire and Water

Deities Bran, Apollo, Arianrhod, Odin, Lugh, King Arthur

Shield + Foundation

Discrimination + Inner Confidence

Royalty

Willow *Tree of Enchantment; Tree of Witcheries*

Saille
5th consonant of the Ogham Alphabet

APRIL 15TH – MAY 12TH
5th month of the Celtic Tree Calendar

APRIL 23RD – *Gypsy Festival of Green
George, Saint George's Day, patron saint of
England*
MAY 1ST – *Beltane
Second of the witches' Cross-Quarter Sabbaths*

Salix caprea
GOAT WILLOW,
PUSSY PALM

Salix alba
WHITE WILLOW

Salix fragilis
CRACK WILLOW

Spring...

THERE ARE SOME 300 species of willow growing almost everywhere in the world, except Australia. These water-loving trees are characteristic of lakesides, fens, and river valleys, in fact most places that are water-logged or prone to flooding. As well as being the tree most associated with moon magic and enchantment, the willow is also known as the Tree of Immortality for the remarkable ease with which it will regrow from a fallen branch or even a tiny twig stuck into moist ground. Even if the twig is planted upside down, it will still grow, for it can root or branch from either of these ends.

By mid-April all willows in Britain and Ireland are in flower, producing their male and female catkins on separate trees. The male catkins of the Goat Willow, *Salix caprea*, appear earlier than the rest and turn brilliant yellow by March, when they are ripe with pollen. Fertilized female willow catkins eventually break up into fluffy seeds which are carried away in drifts on the wind.

The Weeping Willow, *S. babylonica*, comes from Asia. It only produces female flowers in the UK, so it cannot reproduce. Willow leaves are out by May. They are generally long and thin, but those of the Goat or Gray Willow, *S. cinerea*, are more rounded. The White Willow, *S. alba*, one of the largest willows, takes its name from its leaves, which are covered with silvery down.

Willows are often planted on river banks to prevent erosion and the trees were once regularly pollarded to produce straight poles for making hurdles.

The Crack Willow, *S. fragilis*, is the tree most characteristic of lowland rivers. Its fast-growing, contorted trunk is apt to split under its own weight, hence the name. Crack Willows are also remarkable for the many other plants which grow in their crown.

Osiers, *S. viminalis*, are willow shrubs with long, straight, flexible branches. They are cut to the ground each year to encourage the growth of these long pliant stems. These are very versatile and are often used for weaving anything from lobster pots to dog baskets. Willow wood is light and exceptionally supple. The Anglo-Saxon word for willow, which is *welig*, also means pliant.

An ancient willow pollard still producing a regular crop of straight poles for making hurdles.

MYSTICAL ASSOCIATIONS

To the ancient Celts the willow was the Tree of Enchantment and Mysteries, a feminine tree that was ruled by the moon, with a great influence over the vision-producing subconscious. Being in the company of willows was believed to promote and increase psychic and intuitive powers, making dreams more vivid and more open to interpretation. Groves of willows were considered so magical that poets, musicians, priests, and priestesses would meditate within them to enhance their visionary skills and to gain inspiration and clarity of mind. This practice of exploring inner worlds in sacred groves was known to the Celts as gaining Tree-top Inspiration. The willow was associated in many other cultures with poetic and visionary skills.

Orpheus, most celebrated poet of the ancient Greeks, received his gifts of eloquence by carrying willow branches on his journey through the Underworld. The Druids used wands cut from Goat Willow as protective charms. The transformation from the moon-silvered down of the young Goat Willow catkins on the male tree to the golden sun of their pollen-ripe maturity was deemed particularly magical by many ancient peoples, as was the fact that the buds of the Goat Willow grow in spirals up the branches. Willow continues its association with the arts and the forces of creativity today, providing the fine, hard charcoal that is especially favored by artists.

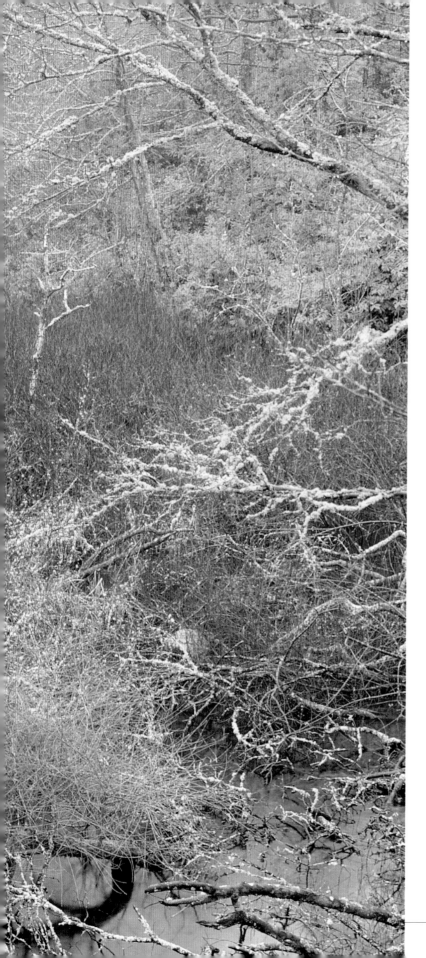

The willow was especially important to healers because of its ability to ease illnesses aggravated by cold and damp.

Rain was considered one of the most precious gifts given by the moon goddess and the magic of the willow – seen as her tree because of its obvious associations with water – was especially revered by rainmakers. It was also, along with elder, the tree most used by healers, the wise women of the Celts, particularly because of its ability to ease illnesses aggravated by the cold and damp, complaints that are common in the Northern European climate. This was the art of sympathetic medicine, in which the conditions a plant favored and its physical attributes were deemed to hold the key to its practical and magical use.

In traditional spells, willow leaves are used to attract love. The Romanies use willow to divine future husbands and an old custom for rejected or abandoned lovers was to wear willow in their hats. To "wear the willow" also meant to grieve openly and willow is still regarded as an emblem of grief. People have always been advised not to burn it as fuel lest sadness befall them. Willow is also associated with funerals. Garlands for mourning were traditionally woven from willow branches and willows were once planted on graves to ease the passage of the soul at death. The ancient Celts believed that the spirit rose from the corpse into the young tree, and that the tree retained the essence of the departed person.

Many ancient goddesses are associated with willows. Persephone, Queen of the Underworld, had a sacred willow grove. The

Greek sorceress Circe had a riverside cemetery planted with willows that was dedicated to Hecate and her moon magic. Hecate, most powerful goddess of willow and water, presided over the magic of the dark side of the moon. Hecate taught sorcery and witchcraft and haunted crossroads and tombs. The ancient Sumerian goddess, Belili, presided over all trees and willows in particular, as well as the moon, love, and the Underworld. Her willow god consort was called Bel. Bel became honored by European Celts as the sun god, Belin, Lord of Life and Death. Great fires were lit in his honor at Beltane, on April 30th and May 1st. These celebrations were once sacred primarily to the moon goddess and her watery, willow magic but as patriarchal sun-god worship ousted the more ancient matriarchal order, so the emphasis shifted away from the mysterious feminine energies of water and the moon toward the more direct masculine approach of fire and the sun. Wells and springs are also honored at the traditional fire and water ceremony at Beltane, which is the second of the four Cross-Quarter Days in the witches' calendar.

The goddess Anatha had a willow cult in Jerusalem, until Jehovah's priests ousted her and claimed the willow as Jehovah's tree at the Hebrew Feast of Tabernacles – a fire and water ceremony that to this day is still known as the Day of the Willows. In Britain, sprays of Goat Willow covered with golden catkins were customarily carried to Christian churches at Easter on Palm Sunday, in remembrance of the branches of palm strewn before Jesus as he entered Jerusalem. This is why the Goat Willow is known as the "Palm Willow" or "Pussy Palm."

Gypsies hold their Festival of Green George on April 23rd, which is also Saint George's Day, patron saint of England. Green George represents the spirit of vegetation. Through the willow and the water spirits, Green George blesses livestock and pregnant women, and heals the young and the old.

The willow reminded ancient peoples of the White Goddess in all three of her aspects; lithe and supple like the virgin, fertile and prolific like the mother, and wizened and hoary like the crone. They were encouraged to recognize in themselves the whole range of emotions, from love and joy, to jealousy and hatred. With its roots deep in the waters of the subconscious and the emotions, the willow is the sacred tree of the visionary goddess, queen of the world of dreams and intuition, of prophecy and psychic powers.

The willow is the tree of the visionary goddess of the world of dreams and intuition, of prophecy and psychic powers.

LESSON OF THE WILLOW

The watery willow encourages the expression of deeply buried feelings, easing sadness through tears and grieving, and teaching the consequences of love and loss in matters of the heart. The willow reminds us of the need to let go sometimes, to surrender completely to the watery world of the emotions and the subconscious, so that we may be carried toward a deeper understanding of our innermost feelings, toward a better appreciation of our hidden motives and secret fears and desires. Any suppressed and unacknowledged emotions can be a major cause of stress and illness. Through emotional expression, and through the sharing of feelings of ecstasy and pain, our ancestors believed they could help heal the human spirit. The willow enables us to realize that within every loss lies the potential for something new.

The willow reminds us to surrender sometimes to the watery world of the emotions and the subconscious.

❦ HEALING ❦

Bitter infusions of *willow bark* have long been used by country people as a remedy for chills, rheumatism, and the hot and cold fevers associated with "ague." Following the ancient principles of sympathetic magic, which state that since willows grow in wet places they will be good for diseases engendered by damp, the natural medicine of the willow has been used to soothe all the aches and pains associated with life in a damp climate, and it has proved most effective. Gypsies make a bitter drink from willow bark for easing headaches and the unpleasant symptoms of rheumatism and influenza.

The active ingredient that makes these traditional remedies so effective, salicylic acid, was isolated early in the 19th century, both from willow bark and from the herb, meadowsweet, which is also a plant that favors damp places. In 1899 acetylsalicylic acid was synthesized and given the name "Aspirin" by the pharmaceutical company Bayer. Since then, it has become the world's most widely used synthetic drug.

Used externally, *willow sap* is said to be good for getting rid of pimples from the skin and a strong decoction made from boiling the *leaves and bark* of willow in water can be rubbed into the scalp to clear dandruff. Willow bark can also be used as an incense to aid deep emotional healing for it clears the head and uplifts the spirits. The *Willow Bach Flower Remedy* restores optimism and faith to those feeling resentment and bitterness. It is used to help those who begrudge and are resentful of others' good fortune, restoring their sense of humor, and helping them to see that "we all have the power to attract good or evil according to the nature of our own thoughts."

❦

Color Silver *Planet* The Moon
Stone Moonstone *Element* Water *Polarity* Feminine
Deities Persephone, Hecate, Belili, Artemis, Selene, Diana, Luna, Athena, Cerridwen, Orpheus, Bel, Belin, Jehovah

Dreams + Intuition
Prophecy + Divination
Healing + Enchantment
Love

Hawthorn *The May Tree*

MAY 13TH – JUNE 9TH
6th month of the Celtic Tree Calendar

Adopted badge of Henry VII (1457–1509), first English king of the Tudor dynasty

Emblem of Estonia and the Buchanan Clan

Crataegus monogyna
HAWTHORN, MAY TREE

❦

Crataegus monogyna 'Biflora'
THE GLASTONBURY THORN

❦

Crataegus laevigata
WOODLAND HAWTHORN, MIDLAND HAWTHORN

When spring turns into summer...

THE HAWTHORN IS a small and elegant tree, perhaps most familiar to the English as a thorny hedgerow shrub. Hawthorns were planted in their thousands by Britain's landowners to seal off their estates behind miles of hedges during the land enclosures between the 16th and 18th centuries. Uncut, the hawthorn will grow up to 45 feet but those growing on exposed moors and downs seldom reach this height. Sheep and cattle love to eat the leaves and young shoots, so most hawthorns are trimmed in some fashion.

The hawthorn's slender trunk and branches become twisted with age. They look their best in winter, seen through moorland mists, clinging to rocky outcrops or gathered in groups on the open hills. The leaves and flowers appear together in May. The flower buds open into little white balls which then unfurl to reveal five pure white – or occasionally pink – petals, each flower being about a ½ inch (1.5 cm) across with a group of pink-tipped slender stamens in its centre. On the back of each flower are five green sepals in the shape of a star. Hawthorns often flower so densely that they form foaming white swathes across the landscape, marking the climax of spring: "the risen cream of all the milkiness of May-time," as the writer H.E. Bates so aptly described it.

When hawthorn is at its peak of flowering, the spring air is heavily laden with a musky scent. The small round fruits, known as haws, turn a deep, wine red when fully ripe in the fall. They, too, bear a pentagram in the center, opposite the stalk. Although they are a favorite with birds, the haws often remain on the tree long after the leaves have fallen, adding a welcome dash of warm color to the early winter landscape.

The leaves are small and a shiny green, with three to five lobes each. The hawthorn is a member of the rose family and there are more than 200 species growing throughout northern temperate regions of the world.

When hawthorn is at its peak of flowering, the spring air is heavily laden with scent. The haws turn a deep red when fully ripe in fall.

MYSTICAL ASSOCIATIONS

In Ireland today the hawthorn is still respected as a tree of enchantment under the protection of the farie realms. Should you sit under a hawthorn on a farie hill on May 1st, you are liable to be whisked away for good to the farie underworld. Lone hawthorns are a common sight in fields and on burial mounds all over Ireland, and to fell one is said to result in the loss of your cattle and all of your money – and even the death of your children. When De Lorean set up his car factory in Ireland, there was a lone hawthorn standing in the centre of the site that the builders had refused to destroy. Apparently De Lorean finally bulldozed it to the ground himself and there was little surprise among his workers when the car plant turned out to be a total disaster.

As a farie tree, the hawthorn guards wells and springs. Even today, hawthorns at such sacred sites are often covered with wish rags, pieces of material tied to the tree to bring luck, love, and happiness. Hawthorn's beautiful flowers are even said to help prayers reach heaven. The tree is a prime symbol of fertility in pagan religion. Traditional May Day festivities are times of contentment and fulfilment, times of courtship, dancing, and lovemaking in the woods. The hawthorn has a potent erotic perfume (said to be reminiscent of female sexual secretions) that encourages acts of love and was thought to enrich fertility. In traditional May Day rites, hawthorn blossom symbolizes love and betrothal. Spring was a time favored for marriage among the Celts and bunches of flowering hawthorn were carried at weddings to bring fertility to the union.

In Britain, one of the first hawthorn goddesses was Olwen, daughter of Giant Hawthorn, the ancient guardian god who was known to the Welsh Celts as Yspaddaden Pencawr. She was the virginal aspect of the White Goddess. White trefoils grew in her tracks wherever she walked. The Welsh goddess Blodeuwedd is also associated with the hawthorn. She was magically created from nine types of flower as a consort for the Celtic sun god, named Llew Llaw-Gywffes. Blodeuwedd represented the light half of the year and the May Queen of traditional Celtic rites of spring is dressed in her image. Such rites celebrated the beginning of new life and the onset of the growing season, as well as the innocent wonder of lovemaking, conception, and birth.

As a farie tree, the hawthorn guards wells and springs. Its beautiful flowers are said to help prayers reach heaven.

The later, more blatantly orgiastic, use of hawthorn corresponds with the cult of the Roman flower goddess Flora. Hymen, god of marriage in ancient Greece, also carries a torch made of hawthorn, and in Turkey, a flowering hawthorn branch is still used as a potent symbol of eroticism. The Italian goddess of hawthorn, Cardea, presided over the natural cycle of childbirth and protected the newborn infants. Hawthorn torches were carried at weddings to propitiate her, since she, like Giant Hawthorn, was opposed to marriage unless sufficient personal sacrifice had been made by the groom to win the bride: then he truly deserved her.

The hawthorn is the tree most representative of the struggles that the Church had to suppress pagan beliefs and celebrations by demonizing ancient practices, especially those connected with sexuality, fertility, and reproduction. The Christian Church's season of Lent, which is a time of fasting and sexual abstinence, runs from the Spring Equinox to the end of May in remembrance of Christ's time in the wilderness. Lent falls exactly at the time when, after the darkness of winter, people were used to joyously celebrating the return of spring, when nature all around is vibrant with re-emergent sexuality and fresh new life. By making this the Christian season

In Britain in 1752 the decision was made to follow the Gregorian Calendar rather than the old style Julian Calendar, which had been the traditional measure of the days and years up until then. As a result, the days between September 2nd and 14th 1752 were omitted because there was by then an eleven-day discrepancy between the two systems. Using the old Calendar, the Hawthorn month would today start more appropriately around May Day (May 1st), which is also Beltane. For country people the seasons were always moveable. For them it was the blossoming of the May tree, not the date alone, which announced the true arrival of spring and the imminent arrival of summer.

The blossoming of the hawthorn gave cause for the celebration of nature's capacity for renewed life.

of abstinence, the Church in effect condemned all ancient sacred festivals associated with this time of year as heresy.

At Glastonbury, seat of the Old Religion, the monks sanctified the hawthorn with an improving tale about Joseph of Arimathea's staff. This was said to have taken root when he stuck it in the ground and has continued to flower both at Christmas and again at its more usual time in May. The original Glastonbury Thorn was cut down by Cromwell's Puritan army, who considered even the new sanctified version to be an abhorrent form of idolatry. However, this was not before hundreds of cuttings had been secretly taken and perpetuated all over England. The Glastonbury Thorn is thought today to be a hybrid of the Mediterranean hawthorn, which does naturally flower in winter and again in spring. Each year, just before Christmas, sprays from one of the thorn trees that still grow in Saint John's churchyard in Glastonbury are sent to the Queen and the Queen Mother. The hawthorn also has a connection with the Catholic Church.

Hawthorn is the tree most representative of the struggles the Christian Church had in suppressing pagan beliefs and celebrations.

Before the Reformation, when Britain was still Catholic, May was considered the month of the Virgin Mary and it was customary at this time to make May altars in your home by surrounding a statue of the Virgin with hawthorn blossom. It is said that the notion that it is unlucky to bring hawthorn into your home stems from anti-papist propaganda from these times.

Hawthorn wood is hard and durable but since the tree is only small, the wood was mainly used for objects such as the handles of personal objects like daggers and knives. The wood of the root is very fine grained and was used for hair ornaments, combs, and trinket boxes. A hawthorn talisman is given as a token of friendship and love, and carrying one was also supposed to protect against lightning strike. The leaves were traditionally scattered in cradles to protect the newborn babies that slept in them.

Henry VII claimed hawthorn as badge of the House of Tudor. At the Battle of Bosworth Field, the crown of England was stolen from Richard III and hidden in a hawthorn bush. From here it was placed on Henry's head instead, making him King of England instead of Richard.

LESSON OF THE HAWTHORN

The blossoming of the hawthorn marks the certain end of the dark days of winter and the return of the procreative forces of nature to the fulness of spring. The beautiful white flowers give cause for celebration of nature's capacity for renewed life and love, and for the wonders of lovemaking, conception, and childbirth. For the Celts there was no shame attached to these natural processes. They were revered and respected as an essential part of life, and as a sacred expression of the human capacity for love.

HEALING

The *flowers, leaves, and fruits* of the hawthorn have properties that reduce blood pressure and stimulate the heart, and which also act as a mild sedative. They are used in herbal medicine to treat heart and circulatory disorders, migraine, angina, menopausal conditions, and insomnia. The *flowers* have the strongest medicinal action. Their excellent sedative effects are used to help people who suffer from angina and palpitations. The *berries* contain both Vitamin B complex and Vitamin C. Crushed and dried, the berries are used by herbalists in decoctions to ease diarrhoea, dysentery, and kidney disorders. A decoction made from the *flowers* may safely be used externally to heal pimples and other skin blemishes. In vibrational medicine *Greenman Essence of Hawthorn* "stimulates the healing power of love," engendering trust and forgiveness and helping to cleanse the heart of negativity.

CAUTION

BECAUSE OF ITS EFFECTS ON THE HEART, HAWTHORN IS NOT SUITABLE FOR SELF-MEDICATION, NOR SHOULD IT BE GIVEN TO OTHERS.

Color Midnight Blue *Stone* Lapis Lazuli *Polarity* Feminine

Deities Olwen, Blodeuwedd, Cardea, Hymen, Virgin Mary

Love + Marriage

Fertility + Procreation

The Heart

Royal Oak

Duir
7th consonant of the Ogham Alphabet

JUNE 10TH – JULY 17TH
7th month of the Celtic Tree Calendar

JUNE 21ST — *Summer Solstice*

JUNE 24TH — *Midsummer Day,*
Saint John's Day

Adopted badge of the Royal House of Stuart

Quercus robur
PEDUNCULATE OAK,
with acorns on
long stalks and
stalkless leaves

Quercus petraea
SESSILE OAK, acorns
without stalks and
short-stalked leaves

Month of midsummer…

THE OAK IS THE tree most associated with England, especially with her navy. It is quite tall with a stout trunk and a rounded, spreading crown. Its branches have a very distinctive way of spiralling toward their ends, which makes the oak easy to recognize in winter. Until the 20th century, the oak's strong and durable timber was at the heart of Britain's buildings, its ships, and its industry. Indeed Britain's past success as a world power is often attributed to the strength and number of its oaks.

Oak wood is also ideal for furniture, glowing golden brown when polished. Acorns were valuable as food for pigs and land was often measured out in terms of the number of swine its oak woods could support, a practice known as pannage. Oaks are particularly long lived and it takes around sixty years for them to produce a full crop of acorns. Those at Windsor Castle are thought to be over 1,000 years old. The oak tree is also renowned for the huge range of wildlife it supports: many insects, birds, plants, and animals depend on the oak for both their food and shelter.

The flowers and leaves appear toward the end of spring. Male flowers form pendulous catkins and the females appear as bud-like spikes. The tender young leaves are at first coral pink, moving through gold to green as they mature. In Britain, oaks produce a second set of leaves around the beginning of August: known as "Lammas shoots," these freshen up the summer canopy. The oak leaves fade through ruddy gold to brown before dropping in fall. Sometimes oaks produce oak apples, hard round balls that appear on the end of its twigs. These house the larvae of gall wasps, which lay their eggs under the oak's bark. The Sessile Oak is the dominant species in the rain-soaked upland woods in the British Isles. The Pedunculate Oak prefers the richer, heavy soils of lowland woods and hedgerows. There are 600 species of oak found in the northern hemisphere.

Britain's past success as a world power is often attributed to the strength and number of its oaks.

Heart of oak are our ships,
Heart of oak are our men:
We are always ready;
Steady, boys, steady;
We'll fight and we'll conquer
Again and again.

DAVID GARRICK, 1759

MYSTICAL ASSOCIATIONS

The oak is the Tree of the Dagda, Lord of Perfect Knowledge and father of the gods of Old Ireland. The Dagda has a great appetite for food and sex, a crude appearance, and a vulgar manner but he protects and entertains without question all those who seek his hospitality. The Dagda is associated with the Magical Caldron of Murias, the Caldron of Plenty, which fed all-comers but appeared empty to any cowards or liars. The Celts were proud of their hospitality. It was their custom first to share their food and entertainment and only afterward to ask the nature of their guest's business, just as the oak, unquestioning and without exception, supports and sustains so much life. The oak is an emblem of hospitality and protection and is still a common name for inns and public houses in Britain.

Symbolic of triumph
through strength
and endurance, the
oak was the tree
most revered and
respected by the
Welsh Druids.

The oak was one of the Three Ancient Marvel Trees of Erinn. Erinn was a goddess of fate, who, like Eire, gave her name to Old Ireland. Irish legend states that in the 1st century CE, at the court of King Conig at Tara, an angel-like being of light arrived from the East bearing a branch on which acorns, apples, and hazelnuts all grew

together. These magical fruits were said to satisfy all of mankind's needs. The angel gave King Conig one of each fruit. Fintan, the Oldest of all Men, and the Hawk of Achill, who were both survivors of the Great Flood, planted the fruits and they grew into the Three Marvel Trees. One of these, the Mighty Tree of Mughna, was an oak that bred true to its parent, bearing successive crops of acorns, apples, and hazelnuts.

The oak was the tree most revered and respected by the Welsh Druids. Symbolic of triumph through endurance and strength, it served as a reminder of the chief's protection and the safety of his shelter. The oak is one of the most widely revered trees in the world and it is a common emblem, both ancient and modern, of earthly and celestial kings. The oak has come to have generally masculine associations, although in ancient times most oracles, including the oak, were deliv-

ered by goddesses. When the religion of the goddess conceded to the patrist rebellion, the attributes of these old goddesses were transferred to the gods who replaced them. In ancient Greek mythology the first tree created was the oak, from which sprang the entire human race. The goddess Diana had an oak cult at Dodona, which was the oldest, most hallowed sanctuary in Greece. Followers of Zeus eventually seized the oracle from Diana and from then on it was the voice of Zeus that was heard to whisper through the oak leaves.

Although it is an emblem of hospitality, the oak is also struck by lightning more often than any other tree and it was seen as a channel through which the sky gods could reach down to the world of man. The Celtic thunder god, Taranis, is associated with the oak, as are the Greek god Zeus, the Roman god Jupiter and Thor, the Nordic sky god.

Esus is the oak god of the Druids and the Celtic counterpart of Zeus and Jupiter. He is the Druidic Prince of Light and his sacred color is white. Revered above all other trees, the oak is said to contain the energy, power, and strength of Esus. The oak was the embodiment of the godhead in nature and a medium for interpreting the will of the gods. It was a doorway to inner spirituality and a pathway to heaven. When the oak accepted the mistletoe it was deemed especially sacred, for the white berries are the sacred color of Esus. They are symbolic of the sperm of the god, an embodiment of the male procreative force of the universe, and they are known to the Druids as "All Heal."

King Arthur's Round Table was made of a single slice of a massive oak and, like Arthur, the oak was seen as a magical protector of England. Merlin worked his magic in oak groves and he is said to have used the topmost branch of an oak for his wand. It was thought possible to contact the ruling deities through acorns, which, because of their resemblance to the head of the penis, were also used in love magic and for the tips of wands made to channel male energies. At traditional May Day celebrations, a character known variously as the May King, the Oak Man, and Jack-in-the-Green dances through the streets wreathed in oak and hawthorn leaves to claim the May Queen.

Charles II, King of England, Scotland, and Ireland from 1660 to 1681, escaped capture after his defeat at the Battle of Worcester in

The oak is the tree of Esus, Druidic Prince of Light. It was seen as a doorway to inner spirituality and a pathway to heaven.

1651 by hiding in an oak tree. He thereafter adopted the oak as his emblem. Charles returned to London and the restoration of the British monarchy on May 29th, which was both his birthday and Oak Apple Day. The day was officially re-named, becoming Royal Oak Day.

In Druidic tradition, the oak is used magically at all ceremonies, especially the quarter celebrations of Solstices and Equinoxes. At the Summer Solstice on June 21st, when the power of the sun is at its height, the oak represents the sun's strength and its ability to ripen the fruits of nature. This is the time of the sacred marriage between heaven and earth, the marriage of the sun god with the earth goddess, when he impregnates her with his future self so that he will be reborn after the Winter Solstice. Fire has long been associated with the oak and it is always the wood used as fuel for the Midsummer Fires. Midsummer Day is the day on which the oak king of the waxing year is sacrificially burned alive to make way for his dual self, the holly king of the waning year. This is also Saint John's Day, being the day on which the saint was beheaded. Midsummer fires are lit in celebration of the oak king's sacrifice at midnight. As in all Celtic festivals, celebrations start on the eve of the day. After his symbolic death in the midsummer fires, the oak king spends the dark half of the year in the constellation of the Corona Borealis, presided over by the goddess, Arianrhod, until his return after the Winter Solstice.

LESSON OF THE OAK

The oak represents courage and endurance and the protective power of faith. The tree's noble presence and nurturing habit reassured ancient peoples that, with the good will of their gods, their leader, and their warriors, they could prevail against all odds. As the Tree of the Dagda, the oak offers protection and hospitality without question, although its true rewards are only apparent to the honest and brave. The ancient Celts deplored lies and cowardice. To be judged mean-spirited could result in exclusion from the clan, which was one of the most shameful and most feared of all possible punishments. Like the oak, we would do well to receive without prejudice all those who seek our help, sharing what we have without resentment or reservation. The oak reminds us all that the strength to prevail, come what may, lies in an open mind and a generous spirit. Inflexibility, however, is the oak's one weakness and the tree is prone to lose limbs in storms. The oak therefore carries the warning that stubborn strength that resists will not endure and may break under strain.

The true rewards of the oak are only apparent to the honest and the brave.

❧ HEALING ❧

The *leaves, bark, and acorns* of the oak are used medicinally, all having astringent, antiseptic, and anti-inflammatory properties. When bruised, the *fresh leaves* can be applied to wounds and hemorrhoids to ease inflammation and promote healing. If soaked in boiling water and allowed to cool, they make a soothing compress for tired or inflamed eyes. The *acorns* make an astringent tonic due to their high tannin content and they are used in old remedies for diarrhoea. Dried and stripped of their seed coat, acorns can be roasted and ground to make a bitter coffee substitute. *Oak apples*, too, were once used in the treatment of diarrhoea and dysentery, hemorrhoids and hemorrhages. The *bark* is the main medicinal part, however. In herbal medicine it is used in decoctions to treat gastroenteritis and severe diarrhoea.

A decoction made from the bark can also be used externally in compresses and in bath preparations to treat chillblains, frostbite, burns, hemorrhoids, and skin diseases, including fungal infections. It will also help to dry sweaty feet. Gypsies use preparations made from the bark as a tonic tea. In vibrational medicine, *Greenman Essence of Oak* is associated with the ability to manifest our goals. It aids the channeling and integration of deep, hidden energy and offers stability to those experiencing the polarities of existence. The *Oak Bach Flower Remedy* is "for those who are despondent but struggle on," nurturing inner strength, common sense, and patience, and improving our ability to take the strain associated with general worry.

❧

Metal Gold *Planet* Jupiter

Stone Diamond *Polarity* Masculine

Deities The Dagda, Esus, Taranis, Diana, Zeus, Jupiter, Thor

Strength + Endurance

Generosity + Protection

Justice + Nobility

Honesty + Bravery

Heather *Flower of Passion*

Calluna vulgaris
COMMON HEATHER/LING

Erica cinerea
BELL HEATHER

Erica tetralix
CROSS-LEAVED HEATHER

Erica vagans
CORNISH HEATHER

Erica ciliaris
DORSET HEATHER

When summer is at its height...

HEATHER IS AN unruly evergreen shrub that grows low to the ground, flourishing especially where there is no natural tree cover on cliff and mountain tops, sand dunes, and lowland wastes, or it is found straggling through the understorey of upland woods, especially in Scotland and Wales. Where it has been managed for grazing and shooting, it forms dense open expanses, which slowly turn the summer landscape lilac pink as the plant comes into flower. Burning rejuvenates heather, just as coppicing does trees. Ling is the most abundant species and it is especially prized by beekeepers for the thick, dark honey that it produces.

Heather has been widely used by heath and moorland dwellers for bedding and thatching, for brooms and baskets, for winding ropes, and for fuel. The flower spikes are used to make beer and they also yield an orange dye. The roots were carved into handles for ceremonial knives, like the Scottish dirk. Heather is a popular emblem among the Scottish clans and the Menzies clan even have a variety named after them, which grows only on a moorland in their territory of Perthshire. Scottish emigrants were so fond of the plant that they took it to America with them, where it has naturalized far outside its usual range.

MYSTICAL ASSOCIATIONS

As summer progresses and heather blooms in ever-deepening shades of pink and purple across heaths, moors, and mountain sides, it is a sight to move even the least passionate of souls. Countless poets and artists have found inspiration in heather's heavenly smell and its color, which is never constant, drifting from pale lilac to red with the play of the light. For the extravagant and emotional Celts, the flowering of the heather heralded a season of rejoicing and self-indulgence. With heather's

> *The king in the red moorland*
> *Rode on a summer's day;*
> *And the bees hummed, and the curlews*
> *Cried beside the way.*
> *The king rode and was angry,*
> *Black was his brow and pale,*
> *To rule in a land of heather;*
> *And lack the heather ale.*
>
> R.L. STEVENSON

Heather is especially prized by beekeepers for the thick, dark honey it produces.

sweet fragrance on the summer breezes and the taste of its rich honey on their tongues, the Celts raised their spirits further by drinking an intoxicating ale made from heather flowers. This brew of ancient legend was the staple drink of the highlands and islands of Scotland, where it was drunk from the horns of cattle. In the ancient Welsh poem *Câd Goddeu*, the "Battle of the Trees,"

attributed to the bard and magician Taliesin, heather is praised for giving "consolation to the toil-spent folk," a reference to the restorative powers of Celtic heather ale.

In midsummer, when heather hums with the sound of millions of bees, the White Goddess herself is often depicted as a queen bee, a *femme fatale* surrounded by a swarm of her male devotees. In this way, heather is a

reality and the world of the spirits, and communicating with the gods. Drinking heather ale at the midsummer celebrations promoted a festive atmosphere, breaking down inhibitions, encouraging the muse of poetry, music, and song to join the company, and invoking the goddess of love. But of course, if drunk to excess, people soon took leave of their senses, passions were unbridled, and tempers flared. Acts of love could soon turn to acts of violence, so it is apt that the reddish-purple of heather is the color of passion. The word for heather in Irish and Scottish Gaelic is *fraoch*, which also means fierce or warlike. Perhaps this is a distant reference to the fighting spirit also evoked by drinking heather ale. The Picts were supposed to have made an especially pleasant and potent brew. In a romantic tale of the massacre of the Picts in the fourth century, the last survivor is said to have plunged to his death over a cliff rather than trade his life for the secret of heather ale.

The flowering of the heather heralded a time of rejoicing and self-indulgence for our ancient Celtic ancestors.

symbol of woman as temptress, as a seducer and devourer of men, the love goddess who couples with the oak king, before he is consumed in the midsummer fires. White heather is considered lucky because it is believed to protect against acts of passion. The bee itself is a Celtic symbol of wisdom, and controlled intoxication was seen as a way of parting the veils between this earthly

A Country Cup
HEATHER ALE

INGREDIENTS

1 gallon heather tops
3½ cups sugar
3½ cups malt extract
28½ pints water
4 envelopes dried yeast

1. Cut the heather tops with scissors when in full bloom, but not overblown, and boil them in 28 ½ pints of water for nearly an hour.

2. Strain through a jelly bag on to the malt extract and sugar and stir until dissolved. Add remaining water and, when lukewarm, add the dried yeast.

3. Cover with a cloth and leave in a warm place for five or six days. Siphon into screw-top bottles, adding one teaspoon of sugar to each.

4. Leave until clear before drinking and always decant carefully into a jug to avoid sediment. Heather ale takes longer to clear than other ales, so be patient. *Wilma Patterson*

LESSON OF THE HEATHER

Heather is a symbol of passionate love, of sacrifice, and self-control. In the first place, heather represents enthusiasm and sensual pleasure, and the benefits that can be enjoyed from spontaneous self-expression. But within this lust for life and exhilaration lies a deeper lesson of the consequences that may arise out of unbridled passion. The Celts believed that you are always totally responsible and accountable for the outcome of your actions, so you were wise to be sure of your own true nature before totally abandoning yourself to the potent delights of heather ale and the pleasures that it could bring. Unchecked, heather is short-lived and unproductive but if burned yearly to the ground, it re-grows with fresh vigor. The lesson of the heather is that a necessary balance must exist between self-expression and self-control for both to be enjoyable and effective.

Purple heather is a symbol of unbridled passion and its consequences.

HEALING

As a medicinal plant heather is used mainly
in the treatment of nervous complaints and
cardiac palpitations, migraine, and problems
associated with menstruation. A decoction
made from the *flowering tips* is said to have
antiseptic and diuretic qualities, and when
added to the bath, it can help to tone up the
muscles and soothe rheumatic pains. The
Heather Bach Flower Remedy is useful for
people have become so self-obsessed that
they have no thoughts or time to give to
others. It promotes generosity of spirit and a
better awareness of other people's problems
and needs.

Color Red

Planets Mars, Venus *Stone* Garnet

Polarity Feminine

Deities Uroica, Venus, Erycina,

Cybele, Isis

Passion

Holly *Tree of Sacrifice*

Tinne
8th consonant of the Ogham Alphabet

When first fruits begin to ripen...

JULY 18TH – AUGUST 4TH
8th month of the Celtic Tree Calendar

AUGUST 1ST – *Lughnasa, Celtic festival of the sun god Lugh*

AUGUST 1ST – *Lammas, Anglo-Saxon Feast of First Fruits, observed by the consecration of bread made from the first ripe corn*

AUGUST 1ST – *Lammas, Third of the witches' Cross-Quarter Sabbaths*

Death of the God of the Waxing Year: birth of the God of the Waning Year.

Ilex aquifolium
COMMON HOLLY
Other common names: *HOLLIN, HOLM, HULVER*

Ilex opaca
AMERICAN HOLLY

THE HOLLY IS A compact, evergreen tree best known for its spiky evergreen leaves and red berries. It generally flowers between May and August but individual trees may begin to produce small, white, four-petalled flowers as early as January and at other quirky times of the year. By fall, female trees are densely covered in scarlet berries. Some trees are soon stripped of fruit by hungry birds, others may carry their berries right through to summer. The more tender branches of the holly are commonly lopped for cattle feed or trimmed by passing deer, giving the tree a neater outline than it would otherwise have.

> *The holly and the ivy,*
> *When they are both full-grown,*
> *Of all the trees that are in the wood*
> *The holly bears the crown.*
> TRADITIONAL CHRISTMAS CAROL

Left to their own devices, holly trees tend to straggle with age until taller branches eventually descend like a waterfall around the trunk, creating a circular evergreen bower that provides year-round shelter from the elements. The holly is also remarkable for its unusually pale gray-brown bark, which is wonderfully smooth over most of the trunk but that wrinkles like skin around the areas where branches grow, forming a puckered hole from which the branch protrudes. Holly is a traditional hedgerow tree; if they are regularly trimmed, hollies quickly form a dense stock-proof barrier.

The English or Common Holly, *Ilex aquifolium*, is found in Western and Southern Europe, North Africa, and Western Asia, as well as in England.

Holly's shiny evergreen leaves made it seem invulnerable to the passage of time.

Only female trees have berries.

Holly is closely linked with the notion of unconditional love, with sacrifice and reincarnation.

MYSTICAL ASSOCIATIONS

The holly is a tree with strong masculine associations that has long been used as a symbol of the potent life force of nature. Holly is connected with ancient sacred rites of birth and reincarnation, and with initiation into the Mysteries. It is closely linked with the notion of unconditional love and, over time, the holly tree has come to represent all sacrificed gods. Holly is generally regarded as a protective tree with close connections to the farie realms and, as with all farie trees, it is considered most unlucky to fell one. Holly was believed to ward off evil influences and to protect against lightning strike, so it was often planted beside houses. It is considered especially lucky for men, who are said to become irresistible to women if they carry a holly leaf or berry about with them.

In ancient times, Britain is said to have been guarded by a giant called Gogmagog. He was a wild and untameable character, clad in leaves and branches, who wielded an enormous club and strode the earth. Fertile and blatantly erotic, he was the spiritual representation of the procreative forces of instinctive nature, brimming with strength and sexuality. Over time, this primeval deity evolved to become the Holly God and later, with much reduced powers, he was eventually known as the Holly King. He can still be seen in all his glory, carved on the chalk hills of Cerne Abbas in Dorset, England. The Holly King is also represented as a giant, covered in holly branches and leaves, who carries a holly bush as his club and who is twinned with the Oak King. In the medieval romance of *Sir Gawain and the Green Knight*, the Holly King appears as the immortal Green Knight, the Oak King as Sir Gawain.

The Holly King reigns over the dark half of the year when the days grow shorter. He ascends the throne after the ritual sacrifice of the Oak King on the midsummer fires. In a neverending cycle of life, death, and rebirth, the Holly King is himself sacrificed at the Winter Solstice, to make way once more for the king of the light half of the year. The Oak and Holly Kings are dual aspects of the guardian god of nature, who in some traditions is also known as the corn god. Their combined role is to protect, court, and make love with the earth goddess, thus ensuring the fruitfulness of the land. Together they are responsible for carrying the green life force of nature through the year.

The Celtic festival of Lughnasa, which falls toward the end of the holly month, commemorates the death of Lugh, god of light and genius, and his subsequent resurrection in the growing seed. Harvest games were held in his honor on August 1st in Britain, Ireland, and Europe. Celebrations traditionally began fifteen days before this date and continued for fifteen days afterwards. The Anglo-Saxon festival of Lammas also falls on August 1st. This was essentially an agrarian feast celebrating the ripening and harvesting of the first fruits of the year.

The holly is a tree of good omen, whose glossy evergreen leaves appear to make it invulnerable to the passage of time and the seasons. Thus holly's evergreen leaves have represented immortality to mystics down the ages. Symbolic also of the tenacity of life, even in the midst of death, holly has been used in summer and midwinter religious observances from the earliest times. Holly was especially sacred to the Druids, who advised people to bring it into their homes in winter. Besides lifting the spirits with its bright red berries and shiny leaves, elves and faries could spend winter in its shelter – at this time of year they did not cause mortals harm. However, any holly brought into the house had to be removed by Imbolc Eve (January 31st), for any leaf remaining would bring misfortune.

In the later Christian tradition, Twelfth Night was appointed for the removal of all greenery. In Christian legend, it was holly that sprang up from under Christ's feet as he walked the earth, the thorny leaves and bright red berries symbolizing his suffering and his blood. Thus, over time, holly has become a prime symbol for sacrificed gods.

The well-known traditional carol *The Holly and the Ivy* – although today generally associated with the crucifixion of Jesus Christ – in fact has its roots in paganism, for holly and ivy represent the male and female principles of life. Yule, which in Britain eventually became synonymous with Christmas, was an old Nordic feast lasting twelve days and beginning toward the end of November. At Yuletide, it was customary for a boy dressed in holly and a girl dressed in ivy to parade hand-in-hand through the streets, leading the old solar year into the new. They symbolized the god and goddess taking the evergreen quality of nature through the darkest time of the year, encouraging the return of the sun and the growth of vegetation. Holly leaves and red berries represented the phallus and the direct fiery energy of the life-giving sun god, and entwining ivy represented the embracing goddess, receptive, and full of potential for new life, spiralling round her partner following the cycles of the moon. So powerful and popular were the pagan rites that were centered around the winter solstice that the Christian Church eventually aligned the birth of Christ to coincide with these traditional celebrations.

Holly wood burns easily and makes a very hot fire. Charcoal made from holly was used by blacksmiths to forge swords and axe-heads – so intense was its heat – while the wood was used to make spear shafts and chariot wheels. The wood of holly is very hard and durable. Holly also has associations with the planet Saturn. In ancient Italy, it was used to symbolize goodwill and happiness during the Saturnalia, a festival that lasted seven days from December 17th to the 23rd. During this time the traditional roles were reversed within the home so that masters served their own slaves and everyone exchanged gifts with each other.

Holly has been used as a symbol of the tenacity of life, even in the midst of death, since earliest times.

Like the Hanged Man of the Tarot, holly represents personal sacrifice in order to gain something of greater value.

LESSON OF THE HOLLY

Holly reminds us of the need to calm our emotions, if we are to reach wise decisions about our situation. The often painful consequences of our actions are brought to the surface for examination, and calm acceptance of our responsibility is required. We are reminded of the need to view ourselves, as well as others, in the light of compassion and unconditional love. Like the Hanged Man of the Tarot, holly represents personal sacrifice in order to gain something of greater value.

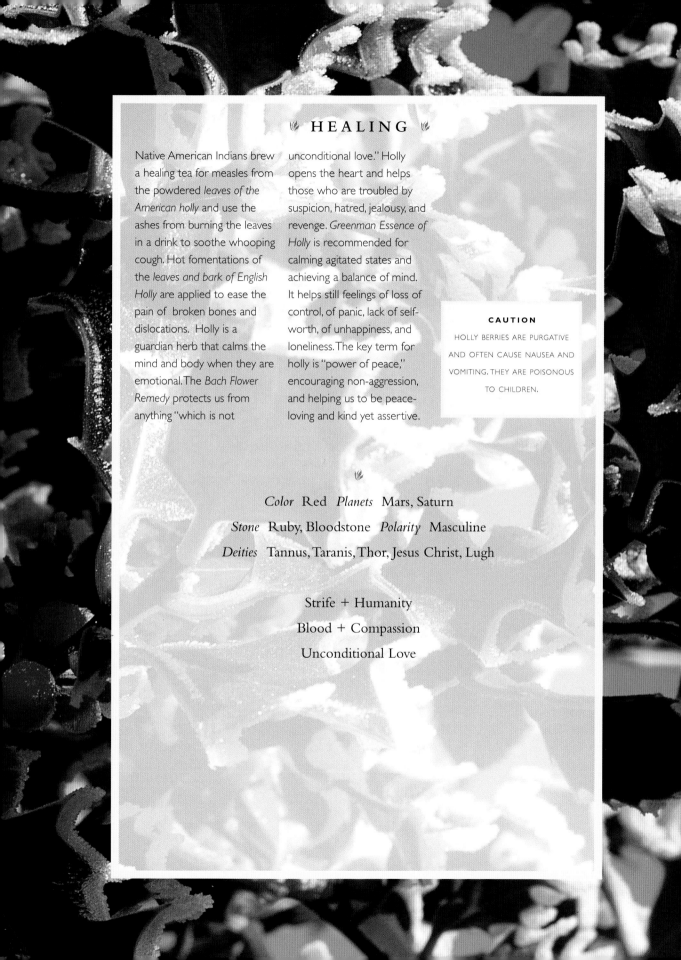

✿ HEALING ✿

Native American Indians brew a healing tea for measles from the powdered *leaves of the American holly* and use the ashes from burning the leaves in a drink to soothe whooping cough. Hot fomentations of the *leaves and bark of English Holly* are applied to ease the pain of broken bones and dislocations. Holly is a guardian herb that calms the mind and body when they are emotional. The *Bach Flower Remedy* protects us from anything "which is not unconditional love." Holly opens the heart and helps those who are troubled by suspicion, hatred, jealousy, and revenge. *Greenman Essence of Holly* is recommended for calming agitated states and achieving a balance of mind. It helps still feelings of loss of control, of panic, lack of self-worth, of unhappiness, and loneliness. The key term for holly is "power of peace," encouraging non-aggression, and helping us to be peace-loving and kind yet assertive.

CAUTION

HOLLY BERRIES ARE PURGATIVE AND OFTEN CAUSE NAUSEA AND VOMITING. THEY ARE POISONOUS TO CHILDREN.

✿

Color Red *Planets* Mars, Saturn

Stone Ruby, Bloodstone *Polarity* Masculine

Deities Tannus, Taranis, Thor, Jesus Christ, Lugh

Strife + Humanity

Blood + Compassion

Unconditional Love

Hazel *Tree of Knowledge*

AUGUST 5TH – SEPTEMBER 1ST
9th month of the Celtic Tree Calendar

AUGUST 20TH – *Saint Philibert's Day, origin of filbert, the American term for hazelnut*

Corylus avellana
'COBNUT' –
ENGLISH HAZEL

Corylus americana
'FILBERT' –
AMERICAN HAZEL

Hazel poles are extremely useful – they will twist and bend without breaking and can even be tied into knots.

Beginning of the nutting season...

THE HAZEL IS ONE of the first trees to come into flower, beginning to blossom in early January. Both male and female flowers are produced on the same plant, appearing long before the leaves. Female flowers are tiny bud-like spikes with protruding red styles and the male flowers are the familiar pendulous sulfur-yellow catkins, which add an early splash of color to the winter landscape.

There are around twelve species of hazel distributed throughout northern temperate regions. Usually recognizable as a woodland shrub with a compact, rounded appearance, hazels will in fact develop into reasonably sizeable trees if not dwarfed by others. If branches are broken off or die, hazels have the ability to send up straight, new shoots from the base of the tree – a habit known as self-coppicing. For some 4,000 years since Neolithic times, people have exploited this habit, deliberately cutting hazels back to the ground to encourage the production of fresh straight branches, known as poles, which can be put to a host of uses. They can be split lengthwise and will twist and bend without breaking. They can even be tied into knots. Usually they were woven into a simple lattice-work known as wattle, which could be used for hurdles and fencing, for walkways across marshes and for reinforcing river banks, for the foundations of buildings and, when filled with mud and straw, for the walls of the buildings themselves. In Britain hazels have proved so useful that old trees are almost always coppiced.

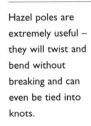

Hazels come into leaf relatively late. The leaves are rounded with a serrated edge and have a soft velvety texture. In the fall they turn many shades of yellow and pink. The nuts ripen from mid-August to October. Each nut is enclosed by a distinctive ragged, leafy frill. It is said to take nine years for a hazel to produce a full crop of fruit. Nine is the number sacred to the Muses and this is one of the many reasons why the hazel is anciently associated with the inspiration behind the arts and sciences.

The hazel is a tree of white magic and healing, of science and poetry.

MYSTICAL ASSOCIATIONS

The ancient Celts regarded the hazel as the Tree of Knowledge. All knowledge and understanding was bound, sweet and concentrated, in the hazelnut's kernel, so all wisdom was combined, as the saying goes, "in a nutshell." The hazel is a tree of white magic and healing. It is a poet's tree, whose sacred nuts conferred inspiration and immortality and were the food of the gods. Our ancestors revered poetry as the highest form of art and magic. In ancient Irish law, commemorated in the Triads of Ireland, the deliberate felling of a hazel carried the death penalty, the apple being the only other tree accorded with such high status:

"Three unbreathing things paid for only with breathing things:
An apple tree, a hazel bush, a sacred grove."

Legends concerning the hazel are most prolific in Ireland. Myths of hazels of inspiration and knowledge, of science and poetry abound. The sacred trees were most often found growing by fresh spring water, where rainbow-spotted salmon swam. Connla's Well, near Tipperary, was a beautiful fountain, over which nine hazels of poetic art produced flowers and fruit simultaneously. As the nuts dropped from the trees into the water, so the salmon who lived in the well ate them, and however many nuts the salmon swallowed, so that number of bright spots appeared on their bodies. Some legends of Connla's Well describe it as being under the sea and the source of the River Shannon.

The air surrounding hazel trees is said to be magically charged with the quicksilver energy of exhilaration and inspiration.

The Salmon of Wisdom, the father of all salmon, was drawn to the well when first going to sea. Each of the well's nine hazel guardians dropped a nut into the water. All the knowledge of the arts and the sciences was conferred with the eating of these nuts and, on swallowing them, the salmon received the gift of wisdom. Touched by the spirit, the Salmon of Wisdom then returned from the sea and swam upstream to the pool where it was born, thus setting the migratory pattern for salmon ever after.

MacColl, which means "son of the hazel," was one of three brothers, the last of the godlike race, the Tuatha De Danann, who once ruled Old Ireland. MacColl and Mac Ceacht, son of the plow, and Mac Greine, son of the sun, were married to three ancient goddesses, Banbha, Eire, and Fodhla. The great Irish hero, Finn MacColl, also bears the name of the sacred tree. Legend tells that his Druid master captured the Salmon of Wisdom and planned to eat it to gain knowledge of all that was happening in Ireland. While preparing the dish for his master, Finn burst a blister on the side of the cooking salmon with his thumb. To soothe the pain, he put his burned thumb in his mouth and thus Finn received the fish's gift in place of his master. In the legend of the Ancient Dripping Hazel, the tree dripped a poisonous milk from limbs that bore no leaves and which were the roost for ravens and vultures, dark birds of divination. Finn MacColl used the wood of the dripping hazel as a shield and its noxious vapors killed

thousands of his enemies. Finn's shield is an emblem of all satirical poems that carry a curse. Such verses were greatly feared and their effect on the subject often led to death. Druid masters are said to have chewed hazelnuts as a means of focusing the mind before uttering such devastating satire and also as a way of obtaining knowledge of things hidden or lost.

The hazel is associated with Mercury, messenger of the Gods, whose gifts were the qualities of eloquence, heraldry, inventiveness, and cunning. Mercury carried a hazel staff, around which two ribbons twined like snakes. This is the caduceus, the symbol of the healing arts still in use today. Mercury's hazel wand also symbolizes the arts of divination and communication. He taught the skills of cultivation and flying and offered protection to travelers. Pilgrim's staffs were thus traditionally made of hazel. Ancient Irish heralds carried white hazel wands, as did Aengus, the Celtic god of love. The tree itself is ruled by the planet Mercury.

Hazel is carried as a talisman for a healthy life and for all-round protection. At Beltane and at the Midsummer Solstice in Ireland, cattle were traditionally driven between two huge fires and their backs were singed with burning hazel wands to protect them from enchantment and bad luck. Horses could be protected from enchantment by faries by tying hazel twigs into their manes. The hazel has a great affinity with water, but its ruling element is air. The air surrounding hazels is said to be magically charged with the quicksilver energy of exhilaration and inspiration.

DIVINING

Forked hazel wands are used for divining water. They are best cut on Midsummer's Eve. To look for hidden water, grip a fork in each hand and pull them apart until you feel the pressure bite. Focus your intent on the water and you will feel the stick bend back and turn as you pass over an underground source. This method has been used to search for mineral veins and buried treasure. In England, up until the 17th century, a forked hazel wand was even used for determining guilt in cases of murder and theft.

LESSON OF THE HAZEL

The hazel encourages us to seek out information and inspiration in all things and emphasizes the value of the enquiring mind and of learning of all kinds. Just as the hazel concentrates all its goodness and its continued existence in the kernel of its fruit, so we attain wisdom by reducing knowledge down to its purest form and passing it on down the ages. Through meditating on the essence of wisdom, we gain creative inspiration. Like the limbs of the hazel, we must remain pliant in our approach to learning. Concentrated thought in an open mind can, like the hazel, become a connection with the divine source of all things. The hazel teaches us the noble arts of learning, teaching, communication, and healing.

The hazel teaches us the noble arts of learning, teaching, communication, and healing.

❦ HEALING ❦

Hazelnuts are both good to eat and highly nutritious, and their main value today is in cookery. More than 60 per cent of the nut is composed of fatty oils and they are also rich in proteins, sugars, vitamins, and mineral salts, making them a healthy part of any diet. Hazelnuts are widely used in confectionery and the oil expressed from them is used in the kitchen as well as in the manufacture of soap and cosmetics. The *oil* can also be used for lighting and as a machine lubricant.

Medicinally, the finely *powdered nuts* mixed with mead or with water, then sweetened with honey, are recommended for clearing a stubborn cough. The *leaves* are diuretic and contain essential oils, glycosides, and sugars. They have been used in tea mixtures to treat varicose veins and circulatory disorders, to cure fevers, and to ease diarrhea and excessive menstrual flow. The *bark* chiefly contains tannins and organic acids. Externally both *the bark and the leaves* can be used in bath preparations to treat hemorrhoids and slow-healing wounds.

In kinesiology, *Greenman Essence of Hazel Flowers* is used to assist "the flowering of skills." It aids the ability to receive, process and communicate wisdom, and the ability to take in information, and helps all forms of study, bringing stability and focus to the integration of useful information.

❦

Color Orange *Planet* Mercury

Stones Topaz and Pearl *Polarity* Masculine

Element Air

Deities Hermes, Mercury, Aengus

Wisdom + Divination

Poetry + Science

Knowledge + Intellect

Healing Arts

Apple *Fruit of Love*

SEPTEMBER 2ND – SEPTEMBER 29TH
10th month of the Celtic Tree Calendar

SEPTEMBER 22ND — *Autumn Equinox*

Malus sylvestris
CRAB APPLE

Malus domestica
ORCHARD APPLE

Time of plenty...

THE CRAB APPLE is the ancient mother of all orchard apples, of which more than 6,000 named varieties have been raised over the centuries. Many are now lost to time, but around 2,000 types still survive. Wildings, the trees grown from discarded apple cores, still preserve the genetic material of old lost varieties. There are around thirty-five species of true crab apple distributed throughout Europe, Asia, and North America. The sweet-scented flowers open in late spring and are generally five-petalled and white, tinged with pink. The leaves are oval, pointed, and toothed. Downy when young, the leaves of the true crab apple are hairless when mature. The crab apple belongs to the rose family and has thorns that develop from spurs on its branches. The round apples are small, hard, and sour, ranging in color from yellow to deep pink. Although deciduous, some apple trees hold their fruit right through winter. The pulp and juice of pressed apples is used to make cider, the heady alcoholic drink that has sustained farming communities for centuries. Cider apples are grown to have a sharper flavor than eating apples and each variety has its own distinctive taste. Traditionally a single apple is left on the tree to ensure a good harvest the following year. Farm-produced cider is still a matter of great pride and dedication. The legendary American, Johnny Appleseed, dedicated his whole life to apples. Born John Chapman in 1774, he traveled the length of the Ohio River valley, planting, selling, and giving away apple trees, which he raised from seed collected from cider presses in Pennsylvania. As with all trees whose fruits are the basis of alcoholic drinks, the apple tree has close associations with divine inspiration and poetry. Wassailing is the ancient English practice of drinking a communal toast to the trees of the orchard after harvest, giving thanks for the bounty of their fruit. Roasted crab apples are an essential ingredient of the traditional drink.

> *An amaranthine place is faerie Emain:*
> *Beauteous is the land where it is found,*
> *Lovely its rath above all other raths.*
> *Plentiful apple trees grow from*
> *that ground.*
>
> RAGNALL, SON OF GODFREY,
> KING OF THE ISLES

Sweet-scented apple blossom opens in late spring. The fruit ripens in September – the apple month.

> *He led him about, he instructed him,*
> *He kept him as the apple of his eye.*
>
> DEUTERONOMY, CH. 32, V. 10

The apple is a universal symbol of plenty, and of love and love's consummation.

MYSTICAL ASSOCIATIONS

The apple is one of the three legendary magical fruits – hazel, apple, and oak – that together were said to satisfy all of mankind's needs, and which were given to King Conig in Ireland in the 1st century CE. By ancient Irish Law there were Seven Noble Sacred Trees: birch, alder, willow, oak, holly, hazel, and apple. The apple, along with the hazel, was the only sacred tree for which its deliberate felling was punished by death. In the medieval transcript of an ancient Welsh poem *Câd Goddeu* ("The Battle of the Trees"), the apple is described as the noblest tree of all, being seen as the tree that symbolizes poetic immortality.

The apple is a universal symbol of plenty and in most world myths and ancient legends it symbolizes the giving and receiving of love and love's consummation, "the apple of my eye" being a well-known expression for the object of one's desire. To ancient Greeks, Aphrodite was the supreme goddess of love and beauty. Those favored by her were granted beauty and irresistible charm, and whoever wore her magic girdle became the object of love and desire. Like many other goddesses of love, Aphrodite's symbol was the apple, which, when cut in two, reveals a five-pointed star around the core, another of her symbols. Apple blossom, too, carries this five-fold theme, since this is the number of its petals. Greek myth tells of the Apple Orchards of Paradise, which were known as the Gardens of the Hesperides. Here grew an

As the preferred host to the mistletoe, the apple was especially sacred to the Druids.

Apples were the food of the Celtic gods as well as the fruit of love.

As the apple among the trees
of the wood,
so is my beloved among the sons.

THE SONG OF SOLOMON 2:3

especially sacred apple tree with a serpent coiled around its roots. This most sacred of apple trees was the gift of Gaia, Mother Earth, to the goddess Hera on her marriage to Zeus, and it was planted in the divine garden on the slopes of Mount Atlas. The tree was tended by nine fair maidens, the Hesperides, who themselves were representatives of Aphrodite, goddess of love. The Celts knew the serpent coiled around the sacred apple's roots as the goddess Cerridwen and in Greek and Celtic, as well as Norse mythology, the fruit of the sacred apple conferred immortality. Nemesis, goddess of divine retribution, carried an apple branch, which she gave as a gift to heroes so their names should live on for ever. Her name is derived from the Greek word for grove, which is *nemos*. The myth of the serpent and the apple also appears in the Bible set in the Garden of Eden. Here it has a very different interpretation, however, in which the serpent actually comes to represent all evil in the

world, woman became temptress and the apple, which conferred the knowledge of good and evil, was the key to humankind's fall from grace.

In Western legend, the orchards of paradise are known as the Isles of the Blessed, where the Tree of Knowledge grows, which bears three sacred apples. Apples were the food of the Celtic gods as well as the fruit of love. As the preferred host of the mistletoe, the apple was especially sacred to the Druids. In Druidic lore the essence of the three sacred apples growing on the Tree of Knowledge came from three drops that fell from Cerridwen's caldron, drops that originally descended from heaven. These three drops are symbolic of the three pillars of the cabalistic Tree of Life, which represent male and female aspects and their "united expression." They also correspond with the Druids' most holy symbol, the Three Rays of Light, which pertain to vision, to letters or symbols, and to the understanding of both. The three sacred drops also represent the "juices or inspirations from which all carnal beings derive their life-giving force."

The Celtic ogham Quert, meaning apple, has another deeply hidden magical significance. The letter Q does not, in fact, appear in the Irish alphabet. It was written by the scribes as CU, a combination of hazel and heather. *Cu* in Old Irish means wolf or hound, a common synonym for the Celtic warrior, which is found in the names of great Celtic heroes like Cuchulain. So Q is found on a deeply hidden spiritual level and this, for the Celtic initiates, was the deeper meaning of Quert, the apple – a spiritual warrior unafraid to face death, who will journey to the Otherworld in order to follow his or her quest. In medieval texts, Quert is described as offering shelter not only to wild hind but also to lunatics. This is perhaps a reference to the shape-shifting shaman, to magicians like Taliesin and Merlin, and to the divine madness that is associated with magical transformations and Otherworld journeys.

In legend, Otherworld visitors to this world often appear carrying an apple branch, coming themselves from places of enchantment where plentiful apple trees grow. In the Voyage of Bran, the warrior god so dear to the Welsh is lured on his adventures by a woman of the Otherworld who appears bearing an apple branch. She is an aspect of the White Goddess summoning Bran to enter the paradise of farie Emain, the amaranthine apple orchard, Land of Eternal Youth. Merlin, too, speaks of the Queen of Farie, who gives out apples to bestow the gift of prophecy. And of course there is Avalon, sacred Isle of the Apple Trees, where Arthur, King of the Britons, was taken when close to death to be healed of his grievous wounds – Avalon, said to be centered around Glastonbury in Somerset, with its mystical tor surrounded by ancient apple orchards, which long ago were themselves encircled by the sea. The name Avalon is said to be derived from the Old Irish word *abhlach*

(pronounced avaloch), meaning "place of the apple trees."

Apple wood is carried as a talisman to attract love and long life and apples are an important ingredient in spells of love, immortality, and healing. Apples are used at the Celtic festival of Samhain (Hallowe'en) to ensure an atmosphere of trust and friendship. The game of apple bobbing is a relic of this ancient practice.

LESSON OF THE APPLE

The apple teaches the lesson of love and faith, generosity and gratitude. Love not just between man and woman but as the driving force behind our existence and the relationships that we share with others; faith both in ourselves and in others; and generosity and trust in the understanding that a heart that is open to give and receive is both the gateway to personal happiness and fulfillment and the key that unlocks the secrets of the Otherworld. The generous apple satisfies body, mind, and spirit, and warns against miserliness, for like attracts like. What we give will be the measure of all we receive.

Apple trees were often planted outside houses to give protection and bring love into the household.

✤ HEALING ✤

With a natural detergent in the *peel* and with *fruit* packed with vitamins, amino acids, sugars, malic and tartaric acids, and mineral salts, the apple has always had a reputation as a healthy food and preventive medicine. Everyone knows that an apple a day keeps the doctor away. The *raw fruit* of the apple is recommended as an aid in the healing of an enormous range of ailments, especially those to do with detoxification, such as gastric and kidney complaints, infections of the intestine, hypertension, gout, and bronchial diseases. Eating raw apples is good for the teeth, keeps the bowels regular, and aids conditions aggravated by mineral deficiency. Apple is said to be beneficial for asthma sufferers, for easing general aches and pains, soothing mental fatigue, and even for reducing cholesterol in the blood. In vibrational medicine, the key term for apple is detoxification. *Greenman Apple Tree Essence* is recommended for transforming negative emotions. It helps the elimination of toxins and brings in spiritual energies that make it easier for us to accept our faults. In the *Bach Flower Remedies*, crab apple is "the cleansing remedy for mind and body for those who have done something contrary to their true nature and who are ashamed of themselves."

✤

Planet Venus

Stone Emerald *Polarity* Feminine

Element Water

Deities Gaia, Aphrodite, Venus, Hera, Pomona, Nemesis, Astarte, Ashtaroth, Ishtar, Cerridwen, Olwen, Gwen, Arwen, Shekinah, Pomona, Freya, Iduna

Faith + Gratitude

Love + Trust

Generosity + Abundance

Self-esteem

Works of Destiny

Aspen *Whispering Tree*

Eadha
4th vowel of the Ogham Alphabet

SEPTEMBER 21ST
Autumn Equinox

OTHER COMMON NAMES

Test Tree, Quivering Tree

Populus tremula
COMMON ASPEN

Populus tremuloides
AMERICAN ASPEN,
QUAKING ASPEN

Moving into the dark...

THE COMMON ASPEN is the smallest, slowest-growing, most delicate member of the poplar family. It grows throughout temperate Europe and Asia, and in China and Japan. The Quaking Aspen, *P. tremuloides*, is one of the most wide-spread trees in North America, distributed from the Atlantic to the Pacific Coast, and is most abundant in the West where it is common to upland forests. Aspens thrive on heavier, poorer soils, especially in damp woods and on river banks. They are intolerant of the shade of other trees. By sending up suckers from the base of the tree, which can themselves become new trees, aspens form strands of genetically identical trees, clones of the parent tree, all joined together at the roots. The common aspen is short-lived, reaching perhaps sixty years of age. It can grow up to around 60 feet tall (20 m), but after fifty years or so the heartwood starts to soften and decay.

The bark is a pale ghostly gray, becoming marked with distinctive black diamonds. Short fluffy catkins appear in early spring. The female flowers have purple stamens, the males red. The tree's most remarkable feature is its leaves; produced after the flowers, they are hairless except when very young and are almost round, and have edges cut with large rounded teeth. Aspen leaves are waterproof and have two minute, resin-lined cups at the bottom of the leaf blade, which catch and absorb moisture. The long leaf stalks are completely flat and they grow at right angles to the blade of the leaf, making them catch the slightest breeze so that they tremble and flutter with a soft, rustling, whispering sound. In fall aspen leaves turn bright yellow, sometimes also red, before dropping to the earth and fading to black.

Aspen leaves tremble and flutter in the slightest breeze, making a soft whispering sound.

The aspen is associated with death and the Underworld, with regeneration and the cycle of the seasons.

MYSTICAL ASSOCIATIONS

The aspen is sacred to Persephone, goddess of regeneration and the Underworld, who was reputed to have a grove of poplars in the Land of Sunset in the West. In Greek legend, Persephone was abducted by Hades, Lord of the Dead, who took her to the Underworld. Persephone's mother, the earth goddess Demeter, mourned the loss of her daughter and searched for her everywhere. When she discovered where she was, Demeter decreed that no seed would grow until Persephone was returned. Because the earth now lay bare, Zeus intervened and instructed Hades that Persephone should live with Demeter for two-thirds of each year, returning to the Underworld for the remaining third. Thus the cycle of the seasons was formed. Seeds and plants flourished until each new winter, when the goddess of regeneration returned to the Underworld and the earth lay dormant. By wearing a crown of her sacred poplar leaves, legendary heroes gained Persephone's protection and were able to enter and return safely from the Underworld.

Our ancient ancestors believed that the wind was the messenger of the gods and anything closely attuned to it, like the aspen, was considered sacred. The aspen trembled most because it had the most acute hearing of all trees, moving continuously in response to a divine calling.

> *The only thing we have to fear is fear itself.*
> FRANKLIN D. ROOSEVELT, INAUGURAL ADDRESS, 1933

To the superstitious this connection with death and the Underworld made aspen an unlucky tree. A wand of aspen, known as a fe, was used to measure bodies and graves, and people feared a baleful charm should they be struck with it. The aspen's connections with the seasons and with rest and regeneration were often overlooked. Church propaganda reinforced the aspen's morbid associations by stating that the aspen trembled in sorrow at the memory of its wood being used in Christ's crucifixion.

Many fearful and paranoid people heard only ill whispered by the wind through the aspen leaves. But this is the lesson of the aspen, the overcoming of fear – the fear of death, the fear of the unknown, even the fear of fear itself. The aspen was, in fact, one of the trees most favored by the Irish Celts for making shields. They called aspen a shield tree, not only for the physical protection that the wood offered but also because, when the lesson of the aspen has been fully learned, the tree also shields the initiate on a spiritual level from the darkness associated with the fear of the unknown. Incense made from poplar is often burned for protection during Hallowe'en (Samhain), at the time when the veils between this world and beyond are at their most thin, and when old fears and outworn things are cast off in order to move on into the fresh new year.

Our ancestors believed that the wind was the messenger of the gods. Anything closely associated to it, like aspen, was deemed sacred.

LESSON OF THE ASPEN

As the wind passes through the aspen leaves, they whisper a message of peace: listen within yourself and find comfort in the still, small voice of calm; in the music of the spheres; in the resounding "om" of existence; in the voice of God – whatever you chose to call the spirit moving through the silence within us. You can interpret this in whichever way is most personal to you. The aspen teaches the lesson of fearlessness, and gives us the strength to face fear that comes with the unknown. To quote Dr. Bach, aspen helps us to understand that "the power of love stands behind and overcomes all things." Once we know this to be true, "we are beyond pain, suffering, care, worry, and fear, and we become participants of true joy."

☙ HEALING ❧

Aspen *buds* are used to produce an essential oil and bitter compounds. Their action is diuretic, antiseptic, and anti-inflammatory. They are used in an infusion to treat infections of the urinary tract, enlarged prostate glands, gout, and rheumatism. Native American women drink aspen *leaf* tea to relieve menstrual cramps. This tea also alleviates diarrhea and urinary disorders. A poultice made from the *root* of the aspen helps heal cuts and bruises.

❧

Planets Pluto, Mercury, Saturn

Stone Black Opal

Polarity Feminine

Deity Persephone, Hades

Listening

Overcoming Fear + Fearlessness

Shield

Light in Darkness

Entwining Ivy

Gort
11th consonant of the Ogham Alphabet

SEPTEMBER 30TH – OCTOBER 27TH
11th month of the Celtic Tree Calendar

Hedera helix
COMMON IVY,
ENGLISH IVY

As the nights draw in...

ALTHOUGH IVY IS usually regarded as a climber, it is as happy trailing across the woodland floor as it is climbing trees and masonry. Ivy stems clamp themselves onto their host plant with a mat of roots that have sucker-like adhesive pads. Ivy has been known to climb up to 100 feet. Like the grape vine, it is not a parasite; it does not directly feed off its host, using it only as a means of support and not putting out true feeding roots until the plant encounters soil.

Evergreen *Hedera helix* has glossy dark-green leaves with paler veins. The leaves on non-flowering stems have three to five lobes, while those on flowering stems are ovate with a pointed end.

The flowers of the ivy are the last main source of nectar and pollen for the bees, first appearing in the early fall and continuing well into winter. They are produced in rounded clusters and are small, with five sepals, five yellow-green petals, and five yellow stamens: this five-fold signature marks ivy as a plant of the White Goddess. Ivy berries are green and globular, eventually ripening to black.

Ivy's reputation as a killer of trees is not entirely deserved, since it neither feeds off its host nor is it ever a direct cause of death. However, when ivy reaches the top of a tree, it begins to bush out, making the tree more prone to wind damage and sometimes causing limbs to break through the sheer weight of its foliage. In this way ivy can eventually smother a plant by blocking out the light that it needs to grow, and so indirectly being the cause of its death.

Ivy was especially popular in Victorian England. It was trained up walls and around windows everywhere, eventually even being grown inside the home as decoration. This began the trend that has made ivy one of the most popular house and garden plants today.

The ivy is not a parasite. It does not feed directly off its host but uses it only as a means of support.

Oh roses for the flush of youth,
And laurel for the perfect prime;
But pick an ivy branch for me
Grown old before my time.

CHRISTINA GEORGINA ROSSETTI, 1862

MYSTICAL ASSOCIATIONS

Entwining ivy represents the embracing and confining female principles of life. Through conception and birth, the male life force is given form by the female body, but in giving life substance so too does woman bring death into being. This association with death as well as life has given ivy a somber reputation. Ivy was the classic plant of the Gothic revival in 18th-century England. As a symbol of melancholy and romantic desolation, it was considered the essential complement to any ruined building.

The white ivy leaf is especially sacred to the ancient forms of the White Goddess, including Ariadne, wife of Dionysus, Greek god of wine, and sister of the Greek wine hero, Deucalion; Pasiphae, Cretan goddess of the moon; Artemis, Greek goddess of hunting and light; and Celtic Arianrhod, goddess of the silver wheel. Ariadne was an orgiastic goddess, in whose honor male human sacrifice was the norm.

Ivy has long been considered to have magical powers and it is closely connected with the vine. It is sacred to Osiris, Egyptian god of magic, to Dionysus, Greek god of wine, and to Bacchus, his Roman equivalent, whose festivities took place in the ivy month of October. At this time, a religious cult of women known as Bacchae, intoxicated by a drink made from ivy, Fly Agaric, and pine sap, ran raving through the countryside, tearing everything that crossed their path to pieces, whether man, child, or beast. Needless to say,

this is not a drink for experimentation. Dionysus had two feasts – the Anthesterion, or "Flower Uprising," during the spring and the Mysterion, which probably means "Toadstool Uprising," in fall. The Greek poet Orpheus, who led the Dionysian rites, was torn apart by such a pack of delirious women. Like the Welsh hero Bran, the head of Orpheus continued to sing and prophesy.

Ivy represents the embracing and confining female principles of life. It is also a symbol of romantic desolation.

earth. In particular, ivy represents the spiraling cycles of the moon, of which there are just over twelve to each solar cycle. Through its influence upon the waters of the earth and female menstrual cycles, the moon governs fertility and the continuation of life as well as death. The traditional Christmas carol *The Holly and the Ivy*, which is seen as a celebration of Christ's suffering, also concerns the differences between expansive male and restrictive female principles of life and the rivalries between sun god and moon goddess, as well as the pulls and influences of the perpetual cycles of the sun and the moon. The rivalry between holly and ivy can, on its simplest level, also be interpreted as symbolic of the domestic war of the sexes.

The Ivy Girl and the Holly Boy were an important part of the midwinter Yule festivities in Britain, when it was customary to dress a girl in ivy to represent the moon goddess and a boy in holly to represent the sun god. They sang satirical songs and competed against each other, before parading hand-in-hand through the streets, together taking the evergreen quality of nature, symbol of the eternal light of life, through the darkest time of the year. In parts of England, the last wheatsheaf to be harvested was also called the Ivy Girl. Bound with ivy, the sheaf was given to the last farmer to finish the harvest and, in this way, ivy became considered a symbol of bad luck. Because of its ability to smother its host, ivy is also used as a symbol of the shrewish wife.

Ivy ale, a highly intoxicating medieval drink, is still brewed at Trinity College in Oxford, England, in memory of a Trinity student murdered by Balliol men.

Ivy's entwining habit also represents the movement and cycles of the heavenly bodies – the stars and planets – and it is symbolic of the knowledge and understanding of the way in which these movements are reflected on

LESSON OF THE IVY

Ivy reminds us of the movement of the heavens and the way this is reflected on earth. It has the ability to bind all things together. It can wander freely, linking tree to tree, or form dense thickets that block out the light and restrict passage. Ivy brings shelter or overwhelming darkness and reminds us that where there is life, there is also death. Ivy represents the wandering of the soul in its search for enlightenment and it carries a warning to be sure of the direction of your desires so that you avoid being ensnared by them. True progress is made, however, when all the lessons of the preceding trees have been linked together with ivy, in such a way that the light can still enter and no limb need break.

Ivy's entwining habit represents the movement of the heavenly bodies and the understanding of their influence on the affairs of humankind.

❦ HEALING ❦

The *young leaves* are an irritant and may cause dermatitis. Their medicinal constituents include tannins, a hederin, organic acids, and iodine. These give ivy expectorant, anti-spasmodic, and cardiac actions. Small doses cause dilation of the blood vessels, larger doses cause constriction of the vessels and the slowing of the heartbeat. Ivy was used in the past to treat rheumatic pain and respiratory diseases. Although not suitable for self-medication, in expert hands ivy is proving useful in modern medicine, being an antibiotic and effective against some forms of bacterial and fungal infection. Because ivy is able to smother the grape vine, it was once believed that its *berries* could overcome the malign effects of alcohol. The berries are purgative in small doses, but the symptoms can be severe if too many are eaten. Although all parts of the ivy are highly toxic to humans, it is often browsed by livestock and it is a widely held belief that sick animals suffering from poisoning will recover if given ivy because of its purgative action. However, this is not recommended to be tried.

CAUTION

ALL PARTS OF THE PLANT ARE POISONOUS. IVY SHOULD NEVER BE USED FOR SELF-MEDICATION OR ADMINISTERED TO OTHERS.

❦

Planet Moon

Stone Opal *Polarity* Feminine

Element Water

Deities Ariadne, Artemis, Arianrhod, Pasiphae, Dionysus, Bacchus, Osiris

The Spirit

Search for Enlightenment

A Warning

Binding + Restricting

Freeing + Uniting

Broom *Physician's Strength*

Ngetal
12th letter of the Ogham Alphabet

Entering the time of dormancy...

OCTOBER 28TH – NOVEMBER 24TH
12th month of the Celtic Tree Calendar

OCTOBER 31ST – *Hallowe'en, Samhain*

NOVEMBER 22ND – *Saint Cecilia's Day,*
Patroness of music and the arts

Emblem of the English Royal dynasty –
The Plantagenets

Celtic Summer's End, Beginning of Winter

Cytisus scoparius
COMMON BROOM,
EUROPEAN BROOM

THE OLD LATIN name for the common broom was *planta genista* but it has since been reclassified as *Cytisus scoparius*. *Cytisus* is a genus of about fifty species of deciduous to evergreen shrubs found in Europe, West Asia, and North Africa and together known as broom. All have pea-like, usually fragrant flowers. The Common Broom occurs throughout temperate Europe. It prefers acid soils, but will survive almost anywhere from high mountain tops to lowland scrub and heath. Broom is a sheltering plant, offering protection from the elements in wild, exposed places. Although it appears delicate, its long straight stems are tough and flexible. They seldom break, bending with the wind, and, as the name suggests, they make excellent brooms. The stems are green, smooth, and five-angled. Younger stems carry groups of up to three leaflets. Broom's golden-yellow, vanilla-scented flowers appear for a couple of months from late spring to early summer. Occasionally the flowers are streaked with red. The seed pods are black and hairy when ripe. Warmed by the sun, they explode open with an audible crack, distributing their seeds into the winds.

There is a rarer low-growing variety of broom, known as Prostrate Broom, which creeps over the cliffs of Wales, clinging stubbornly to the sheer rockface and producing a dense mass of flowers even when faced with the full force of the Atlantic winds.

Broom produces vanilla-scented flowers from late spring to early summer. All parts of the plant have medicinal value.

Previous Page
Clinging to the cliffs
of Wales, Prostrate
Broom flowers in
the full force of the
Atlantic winds.

MYSTICAL ASSOCIATIONS

Broom is a delicate and elegant plant, often appearing in stark contrast to the rough windswept places where it is most often found growing prolifically. Perhaps because it is so distinct from the other plants that surround it (except for its spiny cousin the gorse), broom has long been associated with royalty. Sometimes the ogham Ngetal is also given as the reed, which is an ancient symbol of Egyptian royalty.

Broom was favored as an emblem of nobility by the French medieval lords of Brittany, one of the last Celtic strongholds in mainland Europe. It was the chosen emblem of Geoffrey of Anjou, a French count who married Matilda, daughter of Henry I, King of England. His son ascended the English throne in 1100 CE, to become King Henry II. This was the foundation of a royal dynasty that ruled England for more than 300 years between 1154 and 1485 and that was known as the Plantagenets, taking its name from the old Latin for broom, *planta genista*. A broom with open pods, its seeds scattered, is carved on the robes of King Richard II on his tomb in Westminster Abbey.

Broom is a medicinal plant traditionally used in the treatment of all diseases associated with excessive revelry, whether from too much drinking, eating, or sex. It is well suited to the month of November, often a cold and bleak time of year, when the affluent did little else except make merry to entertain themselves. It was the favorite medicine of that man of singular debauchery and excess, King Henry VIII. The 16th-century herbalist Gerard wrote: "That worthy Prince of famous memorie Henry VIII, King of England, was woont to drink the distilled water of Broome floures against surfets and diseases thereof arising."

Ancient Celtic texts, which discuss the deeper meaning behind the ogham alphabet, underline this link between broom and the healing arts. In the Word Ogham of Morainn, Ngetal is given as physician's strength, *panacea*. In the Ogham of Cuchulain it is the beginning of heroic deeds and healing, and in that of Aonghus it is called the robe of physicians. All parts of the broom have healing potential and therefore close links with Mercury and all deities who preside over the healing arts. The green tips of the flowering branches of broom have a long tradition in herbal medicine and were gathered during the Second World War for use as a mild diuretic. The main medicinal component of broom is sparteine. In very large doses sparteine can create an excited state and hallucinations. This is sometimes suggested as the reason behind the traditional link between the broom and witches, and behind the notion that witches ride through the skies on broomsticks.

Before the introduction of hops to the brewing process, the broom's tender growing shoots were commonly used to flavor beer, with the additional effect of making it more intoxicating. Broom is therefore also associ-

Known as "Physician's Strength," broom is traditionally used to treat diseases associated with excess.

ated with Bacchus and all other gods of wine and revelry. Even sheep have been seen to become briefly intoxicated after eating broom's seed pods. The green flower buds, just before they show yellow, used to be pickled to make imitation capers and the raw open flowers were used in salads. Broom is no longer recommended for general use since the narcotic content can vary enormously from plant to plant, and so in large quantities broom is potentially dangerous.

Tea made from the golden, vanilla-scented flowers is, however, still an approved diuretic. Broom is used magically in spells of purification and protection. It is said to be particularly useful for dealing with poltergeists. Broom is also used to raise winds by throwing it into the air and to calm winds by burning it and burying the ashes.

Broom is a symbol for astral travel, a process described in the language of the shaman and the Druid as Otherworld journeying, whereby a person's spirit leaves the body and travels independently of earthly reality. This links broom with Morpheus, the Greek god of dreams, and with his equivalents from other belief systems. Otherworld experience can be linked to broom's narcotic properties, although intoxication is not in any way essential to astral travel nor to exploring related aspects of the mind outside general experience. Narcotics can open this door, but the effect can be illusory. However, with both great healing potential and narcotic effect, broom has long, firm-rooted associations with healers and magicians, with wise women and shamans.

LESSON OF THE BROOM

Broom reminds us of the importance of caring for our own personal wellbeing on all levels – physical, mental, emotional, and spiritual. Falling at the end of the Celtic year, the month of broom is a time for taking stock, for making a clean sweep, for ridding yourself of unnecessary baggage and harmful habits. In short, broom is symbolic of all the benefits of cleaning up your act. Broom also advises you to pay attention to your dreams.

Broom is an apt symbol for the wellbeing of the whole person – body, mind, and soul.

HEALING

All parts of broom have medicinal value, its *flowers, flowering stems, growing shoots, seeds*, and *roots*. The most important active constituent is the alkaloid sparteine. Other ingredients include scoparin, tannins, essential oils, and bitter compounds.

A decoction of the *young branches or seeds* will cause violent vomiting if taken in too strong a dose. Some of the constituents are now included in modern branded medicines. Medicines containing sparteine are prescribed for heart and circulatory disorders. Sparteine is hypertensive, dilating the blood vessels and raising blood pressure. It stimulates the smooth muscles of the intestines and also those of the uterus, so it is used in obstetrics. Preparations made from broom, when properly controlled, will also relieve conditions such as gout, sciatica, and painful joints, as well as malaria and fever. They can also help break down stones in the kidneys or bladder. *Oil* from the stems has been used to relieve toothache and to clear the head and skin of parasites. *Broom-flower* tea is still used as a valuable diuretic today.

CAUTION

THE AMOUNTS OF THESE SUBSTANCES VARY A GREAT DEAL BETWEEN INDIVIDUAL PLANTS, SO BROOM IS NOW CONSIDERED TOO UNRELIABLE – AND THEREFORE POTENTIALLY TOO TOXIC – FOR GENERAL USE.
NOT TO BE USED FOR SELF-MEDICATION OR ADMINISTERED TO OTHERS. DOSAGE AND TREATMENT WITH ANY PREPARATION CONTAINING BROOM MUST BE PRESCRIBED BY A MEDICAL PRACTITIONER.

Color Blue *Planet* The Moon
Stone Opal *Polarity* Masculine
Element Water
Deities Mercury, Morpheus, Bacchus

Royalty
Cleansing
Healing
Psychic Protection
Astral Travel

Blackthorn *The Mother of the Wood*

Straif

Additional consonant of the Ogham Alphabet

OCTOBER 31ST/NOVEMBER 1ST

Hallowe'en, All Souls, Samhain

Fourth of the witches' Cross-Quarter Sabbaths

Prunus spinosa

BLACKTHORN, SLOE

Parting the veils between the physical and the spiritual...

THE BLACKTHORN IS more of a shrub than a tree, traditionally believed never to exceed a height of more than 13 feet. Its twigs are downy when young with many straight side-shoots that become thorns; these are much longer and sharper than those of the hawthorn. The blackthorn produces vigorous suckers from its roots. These grow to form dense, thorny thickets that are almost impenetrable and tear at the flesh. The blossom appears very early in the year, before the leaves, which are thin and rounded with toothed edges. The small flowers make their first appearance in early March and continue blooming for several months. They are borne alone or in pairs and have five white petals, very occasionally pink, with a crown of red-tipped stamens in their center. The small, globular fruits, known as sloes, have blue-black skin with a grayish bloom and green flesh. They are very tart and bitter to the taste. The dark fruits of the blackthorn mark the beginning of winter, just as its flowers mark winter's end. In Britain March is a time when cold north-easterly winds blow and the rough weather at this season is known to country people as a blackthorn winter. The blackthorn's delicate white flowers are a sign of hope during this harsh time of the year, bringing light into the darkness of winter's melancholy, easing feelings of negativity and depression.

> *There was given to me a thorn in the flesh, the messenger of Satan to buffet me.*
>
> II CORINTHIANS, CH. 9, v. 19

Armed with sharp spines, the blackthorn forms dense thickets which tear at the flesh.

Blackthorn blossom appears very early in the year, marking the end of winter.

MYSTICAL ASSOCIATIONS

The festival of Samhain falls on October 31st, marking the end of the Celtic year. It is the eve of the beginning of winter, ushering in the season of darkness, a time of dormancy when nature stands still. By now all crops should be in, the fruit harvested, and animals brought down to their winter pasture. Samhain is the time when the Dagda, Irish god of nature, couples with the Morrigan, goddess of war and psychic powers. On this night the veils between the physical world and that of the spirits are especially thin and communication with the dead is believed possible. Some say that the dead even leave their graves at this time and walk among the living.

The blackthorn is the sister of the hawthorn. Together they represent the dark and light halves of the year. Both trees are said to have formed Christ's crown of thorns and this was the reason Christian monks gave for their unluckiness. However, blackthorn's sinister associations have older roots, for traditionally it is the tree of black magic and blasting. Its thorns are long, strong, and extremely sharp, proving ideal for piercing the skin. A scratch often leaves wounds that turn septic, and the thorns, when tipped with poison, made a discreet weapon ideal for dispatching enemies. When used in this way, blackthorn was known as the pin of slumber. This is possibly the origin of the tale of Sleeping Beauty, who pricked her finger on a poisoned spindle and fell into a very deep

Of all the trees that grow so fair,
Old England to adorn,
Greater are none beneath the Sun
Than Oak, and Ash, and Thorn.

RUDYARD KIPLING, *PUCK*

OF POOK'S HILL, 1906

death-like slumber. An impenetrable barrier of thorns grew up around her sleeping place, which only the power of love could penetrate. The thorns of the blackthorn were used by witches for sticking into wax images of their enemies as a means of wreaking revenge upon them. But this was not always a vengeful process. It could also be used to protect a person from harm, but this does depend on the intent of the person who is performing the ritual.

Witches used blackthorn wood as a walking stick, known as the black rod, which was believed to cause miscarriage if pointed at a pregnant woman. The devil himself was said to pierce the finger of his initiates with the spines of the blackthorn, and finding such marks about a person's body was often seen as sufficient cause for burning the bearer as a witch. Blackthorn was condemned as the black witch's tool and was sometimes ironically used in the pyres on which witches were burned. When Major Weir was burned as a witch in Edinburgh in April 1670, a blackthorn staff was burned with him as the chief instrument of his black magic.

Blackthorn is the traditional wood for making the Irish shillelagh, a cudgel used by tinkers for fighting at country fairs. The juice of the sloe makes an indelible ink and the whole fruit yields a strong red dye. The color red is synonymous with death in Irish legend. It is also the color associated with Mars which, together with Saturn, is the blackthorn's ruling planet.

LESSON OF THE BLACKTHORN

The blackthorn was respected as a cantankerous old crone, the hag aspect of the White Goddess, whose thorns remind us of our own negative attitudes that tear us apart. These attitudes also take root and grow into impenetrable thickets if they are left unchecked. We are advised to look at the many ways in which we hurt ourselves and others, and to think of ways to prevent this. When we face up to our own negativity, blackthorn guides us through the darker parts of our personality, helping us to pay off spiritual debts, and to accept the inevitability of our own death, which is the one thing on earth of which we can all be certain.

Blackthorn is the traditional tree of black magic and blasting, whose thorns remind us of our own negative attitudes.

HEALING

The *fruit and leaves* of the blackthorn contain
tannins, organic acids, sugars, and Vitamin C.
Steeped in boiling water, the *flowers* have mild
diuretic, tonic, and laxative properties. The
dried fruits are used to treat bladder, kidney,
and stomach disorders.

The liquid from the *boiled leaves* can be
used as a mouthwash and to soothe throat
conditions such as tonsilitis and laryngitis. In
vibrational medicine *Greenman Blackthorn
Essence* is recommended for bringing hope
and joy to the depressed and for stabilizing
emotions. It is also good for problems with
circulation, strengthening the blood supply
and helping the absorption of nutrients.

Color Red *Planets* Mars, Saturn

Stone Black Opal

Polarity Feminine

Deity Morrigan

The Inevitability of Death

Protection + Revenge

Strife + Negativity

Elder *The Elder Mother; The Queen of Herbs*

Ruis
13th consonant of the Ogham Alphabet

NOVEMBER 25TH – DECEMBER 21ST
13th month of the Celtic Tree Calendar

DECEMBER 21ST — *Winter Solstice*

Sambucus nigra
ENGLISH ELDER

Sambucus canadensis
AMERICAN ELDER

Season of mists and darkness...

THE ELDER IS A small tree, rarely reaching more than 30 feet (10 m), although in legend it is said to have grown much taller. More of a compact shrub when young, it becomes a straggling and unruly tree in old age.

The elder prefers lime-rich soil, but it is not fussy, growing almost anywhere and able to produce a mass of flowers and fruit even in dense shade. By June the elder is covered in creamy, flat-topped sprays containing hundreds of tiny five-petalled flowers. They have a delicious smell and a flavor like Muscat grapes. Small green berries form and ripen, plump with juice, to a purple-black color, the fruit hanging down in dense bunches known as drupes.

The elder grows by producing stems from its base, constantly replacing dead wood with fresh new growth. It will also root easily from cuttings – simply break off a twig, stick it in the ground, and it is likely to grow. These habits made elder an ancient symbol of death and regeneration. The bark on the main stems is rough and fissured. On younger wood, the bark is green and much smoother.

The dark spots dotting the surface are pores through which the tree breathes. Young stems are filled with white pith that can easily be removed, leaving a hollow tube that is then ideal for making pea-shooters, whistles, and panpipes.

The pith is one of the lightest natural solids and it is used commercially for holding biological specimens while they are being cut into sections for microscopy. In contrast, the old heartwood and wood from the elder's roots is exceptionally hard and dense. It is white and close-grained and good for turning and making small items like toys and utensils. The elder marks the progress of the seasons. Its young leaves herald the return of spring and the sweet fragrance of the elder blossom announces the true arrival of summer. When elderberries are fully ripe, summer is said to be over, and when elder leaves blush and fall and winter's cold brings disease and discomfort, then the elder's medicines truly come into their own.

The 17th-century English writer, John Evelyn, remarked of the elder, "If the medicinal properties of its leaves, bark, and berries were fully known, I cannot tell what our countryman could ail for which he might not fetch a remedy from every hedge for sickness and wounds."

The elder is able to grow almost anywhere, continuing to produce a mass of creamy blossoms.

The Elder Mother was believed to dwell in the elder tree. She worked a strong earth magic and punished those who used her tree selfishly.

The elder is the tree most often used to undo spells of evil intent.

MYSTICAL ASSOCIATIONS

Numerically the elder is the ultimate tree of the White Goddess, whose prime sacred number is five (the other being three). Each creamy elderflower has five petals, five yellow stamens, and five sepals, which form a tiny green star on the back of each flower. Elderflower clusters hang from five stalks at the end of each branch, which each divide again into five stalklets.

The elder is under the protection of the Old Crone aspect of the Triple Goddess, who guards the door to the Underworld, to death, and to the dark inner mysteries. Elder is especially associated with goddesses of the waning moon and the waning year, in particular Hela, Queen of the Dead.

Throughout northern Europe the elder is associated with death and regeneration and with magic, and it is the tree most often used to undo spells of evil intent. As the tree of the thirteenth month of the Celtic year, the elder is linked with all superstitions that surround the supposed unluckiness of this particular number.

The ancient Celtic race believed that peoples' perceptions and memories of your life in this world would effect the way that you were perceived in the Otherworld after death. It was important therefore to die honorably and with dignity, and that people thought well of a person after they had died. Cowardice in the face of death was most shameful. The belief that it is wrong to speak ill of the dead still persists in many cultures today. Elder reminded ancient peoples of the need for honor and dignity at all times. The Elder Mother, the crone aspect of the Triple Goddess, was believed to dwell within the tree. In Scandinavian and Danish mythology she is called Elle or Hyldemoer. The Germans knew her as Frau Ellen and to the English, she was Lady Ellhorn. She worked a strong earth magic, avenging all who harmed her host tree and punishing those who used any of its parts with selfish intent. According to legend, witches would often turn themselves into elder trees, giving rise to the superstition that if such an elder were cut, the witch would return to human form still bearing the marks of the cut. Such tales fueled the practice of "witch-hunting," effectively making it possible to try and execute as a witch any unpopular woman with a limp or some other kind of deformity.

The enormous medicinal value of the elder was certainly recognized by the ancient Britons, Celts, and Romans, as it probably was by many peoples before them, for the Elder Mother within the tree was believed to cure all of mankind's ills. The Wise Women who practiced the art of healing often took great risks in using elder, with the prospect of being executed as a consort of the devil ever-present. Some members of the Christian Church even decreed that the only proper use of the elder was to seek out the evil of witches. It was claimed that if a baptized person was to dab green elder juice on his or her eyelids, then all the doings of witches in that very community would be revealed to him or her. Perhaps not surprisingly, elder was also said to be both the wood of the Cross and the tree from which Judas hung himself. The stunted and twisted appearance of the tree was claimed to be the result of carrying the weight of guilt and remorse ever since. A strange fungus with the macabre name of Jew's Ear grows on old, dying elder wood. These are said to be the ears of Judas, ever doomed to hear the wind whisper the guilt of his betrayal of Jesus.

Elder is a notoriously bad wood for fuel and there are many superstitions against burning it. It is said that the elder mother will take revenge for such an act by sending plagues of bad luck. Elder has a fearful reputation in English folklore. Burning elder brings death to the family and simply taking the plant indoors is said to invite the devil into the house. In Irish folklore, anyone who falls asleep under a flowering elder might never awaken, for the fragrance of the elder flowers can transport you to the farie realms. If you stand beneath an elder on Midsummer's Night, you might be able to see the King of the Faries and all his entourage. If you carry no protection from this bewitchment, you might be charmed away forever. Farmers traditionally welcome the elder on their land, for it is believed to offer livestock protection from lightning and to promote their fertility. It is also said that if a pregnant woman kisses an elder, it will bring good luck to the baby that she is carrying.

The elder has many practical as well as medicinal uses. Ancient Britons and Celts used elderberries boiled in wine as a black

In Irish folklore the fragrance of elder flowers can transport you to the farie realms.

The Jew's Ear fungus grows on moribund elder – said to be the ears of Judas forever hearing the wind whisper the guilt of his betrayal of Jesus.

hair dye. The roots and leaves are still used in the Hebrides to dye wool black. The bark also yields a black dye. If mixed with alum, the leaves dye green and the berries dye blue, purple, and violet. Bruised elder leaves make a useful insect deterrent and an infusion of elder leaves sprayed about the house will keep insects at bay.

You can also boil the leaves in water and spray plants with the resulting liquid to keep them free of pests like caterpillars, aphids, and mildew. The berries are good in puddings and jams, and elderberry wine was once so popular as a tonic that huge orchards were grown in Kent in the south of England to keep up with demand for the fruit.

Elderflower wine and elder champagne are the best of homemade wines, and one of the most popular with amateur vintners, and elderflower cordial is a enjoyable tonic drink.

LESSON OF THE ELDER

The lesson of the elder is a difficult one. Not only are you asked to accept the inevitability of your own death, but you are also asked the far more personal and potentially embarrassing question – how might you be fated to be remembered, both for good and ill, were you to die today? In the dark days of winter, elder presents us with a mirror in which we must see ourselves truly reflected if we are to die with dignity and without regrets.

Virtually all parts of the elder are useful medicinally. Today primarily the fruit and flowers are used.

❧ HEALING ❧

Elderflowers should be picked on a dry day when they are fully open, with as little green stalk showing as possible. Do not wash them or this will reduce the fragrance. Dry them as quickly as possible, turning them often. To make an infusion, use two teaspoons of dried or fresh flowers to a cup of boiling water.

Cover and steep for ten minutes. An elderflower infusion will ease a fever and soothe the pain of rheumatism and mild nervous disorders like sciatica and migraine. It can relieve many common respiratory complaints like catarrh and bronchitis, and help cure diseases like measles, gout, and rheumatism. Inhaled, it will ease a head cold, and used as a gargle it will soothe laryngitis. It is also useful as a cleanser for conjunctivitis,

being mildly astringent and having a gentle cooling effect. An *essential oil* distilled from elder flowers is used in eye and skin lotions. Diluted as elderflower water, it was once very popular for whitening the skin and clearing freckles, as well as for soothing sunburn and tired eyes.

The healing properties of the *berries* are similar to the flowers, only weaker. Formerly they were used as a cure for syphilis. They are mildly laxative and sedative and contain a large amount of Vitamin C when fresh. A syrup made from five parts of fruit to one of sugar and simmered until it has the consistency of honey can be taken by the spoonful or diluted and drunk to ease bronchitis or influenza.

The *leaves* are diuretic, expectorant, and purgative. They are mildly toxic and can

cause nausea. Their juice has been used to relieve inflammation of the eyes and to clear a stuffy nose. The *bark* of the English Elder is an especially strong purgative, which was used anciently to evacuate and cleanse the stomach and system in cases of poisoning. In vibrational medicine, *Essence of Elder* is used to promote feelings of self-worth. It is especially useful in times of transformation and change, and is good for fretful children.

CAUTION

ELDER LEAVES AND
BARK SHOULD NOT BE
USED FOR SELF-MEDICATION.
FRESH ROOT OF THE AMERICAN
ELDER IS POISONOUS AND
SHOULD NOT BE USED AT ALL.

❧

Colors Black, Dark Green *Planet* Venus

Stone Olivine *Polarity* Feminine

Element Water *Deities* Hel, Hela, Holda, Hilde

Judgment + Transformation

Death + Regeneration

Fate + The Inevitable

Yew *Tree of Resurrection; Tree of Eternity*

Idho
5th vowel and last letter of the Ogham Alphabet

DECEMBER 21ST
Winter Solstice

Death of the King of the Waning Year

Taxus baccata
YEW (EUROPE AND
NORTH AFRICA TO IRAN)

Taxus baccata
'fastigiata'
IRISH YEW

Taxus cuspidata
JAPANESE YEW

The end in the beginning and the beginning in the end...

THE YEW IS exceptionally long-lived, but difficult to age accurately. After 400 to 500 years, yews become hollow, making dating by ring counts impossible. However, recent dating techniques have now revealed that the yew probably has the longest lifespan of all trees. In Britain yews are commonly found growing next to ancient churches. Many are at least as old as the church, others considerably older, in some cases by thousands of years. The ancient yew at Fortingall in Perthshire, Scotland, is now estimated to be around 9,000 years old. Many yews are believed to be at least 2,000 years old.

Yews prefer well-drained, lime-rich soil. They are evergreen with dark-green, glossy needles that grow opposite each other along the branches, like the barbs of a feather. Very little grows in the shade of an ancient yew grove. Yews come into flower early, usually around February, with male and female flowers on separate trees. The male flowers are cone-like and yellow, shedding clouds of pollen in dry weather. Female flowers resemble tiny green buds. The ripe fruit holds a single seed enclosed in a bright scarlet, fleshy cup known as an aril. Birds love them, spreading the seeds in their flight after they've eaten them. Yew seeds are slow to germinate, usually needing two to three years before they will begin to grow. The lower branches of ancient yews eventually reach the ground and take root, forming a strengthening outer trunk that supports the tree and protects its older heartwood. This habit of renewal through transformation, combined with the tree's longevity, earned the yew the name Tree of Eternity.

In hollow trees, the inner wood has the color and appearance of the flesh of a flayed animal, especially when wet, and the tree appears to bleed when cut – qualities that greatly enhanced the sacred reputation of the yew. Yew wood has immense endurance. A 250,000-year-old yew-wood spear found at Clacton in the south-east of England is the world's oldest known wooden artifact. Yew was used to make longbows, hence the species name *Taxus*, from the Greek for bow, *taxon*. It also yields a deadly poison often used to tip arrowheads, making both the arrows and the tree doubly fatal. Yew bows are said to have killed three English kings – William Rufus, King Harold, and Richard the Lionheart.

Yews are commonly found by ancient churches. Many are at least as old as the church, others considerably older.

To the Irish, the yew was the tree revered above all others. It is said to guard the doorway between this life and the next.

MYSTICAL ASSOCIATIONS

One of the Five Magical Trees of Ireland was a yew known as the Tree of Ross. To the Irish Ollaves, the yew was the tree revered above all others. In the mythology of the Tuatha De Danaan, the godlike magical race of ancient Ireland, one of Ireland's last great warrior queens was Banbha, sister of Fodhla and Eire. Banbha was slain and deified as the death aspect of the White Goddess. The yew, as the tree of life-in-death, was sacred to her and was known as the Renown of Banbha. Other ancient Celtic titles for the yew are Spell of Knowledge, which speaks for itself, and the King's Wheel, which is said to refer to a brooch representing the continuous cycle of existence that was worn by Celtic kings as a reminder of their own death and rebirth. The yew was symbolic of this cycle. Through death it opened the door to rebirth and to the eternal life of the soul. The Druids believed that the yew could transcend time. In Druidic initiations, yew represents the high grade of Ovate. To achieve this level of accomplishment, the initiate must undergo a symbolic death in order to be reborn into a new level of awareness, said to be beyond time and its limitations. The yew then becomes a direct link to the tribal ancestors and to the spirit realms, where we are told there are angels, guides, and guardians assigned to help each one of us, if we allow ourselves to be open to their help.

Yew sticks were cast to divine the future and yew rods were used for making long-lasting ogham inscriptions because, when seasoned and polished, the wood endures for thousands of years. The yew's resilient nature thus ensured that the magic imbued by the carved oghams would continue long into the future. Wands and staffs of yew were considered especially potent because of this resilience; they were said to channel the magical power of the spirit of the tree, the might of the gods, and the will of the owner. In legends around the world, a touch from a wand or a blow from a staff could cause great transformations, either for good or for evil. Superstitions surrounding the yew greatly enhanced the magical power of its wood, fed by a general fear of death and an awareness of the fatal uses to which the tree has been put, both as a weapon and as a deadly poison.

The yew is said to guard the doorway between this life and the next and to prevent any interference by evil spirits in the Otherworld. As a sacred Tree of Immortality the yew is anciently associated with places of burial, where it was believed to protect and purify the dead, and in Brittany it is said that the graveyard yew extends a root to the

The yew is symbolic of the sum of all wisdom. Its ultimate lesson is the transcendence of death.

mouth of every corpse buried around it. The custom of putting sprigs of yew inside the shrouds of the dead was similarly believed to protect the immortal soul on its journey through the Underworld. In ancient Greece and Italy the yew was sacred to Hecate, whose cult spread as far afield as Scotland. The famous witches' caldron in Shakespeare's *Macbeth* contains slips of yew, "silver'd in the moon's eclipse," while hebenon, "the double fatal yew," is the poison that Hamlet's uncle poured into the king's ear to murder him. To the Christian Church the yew was the Tree of Resurrection, symbol of Jesus Christ's rising from death after crucifixion. The yew is also under the rule of the planet Saturn and, because of its connection to bows and arrows, it also represents the zodiacal sign of Sagittarius – the archer.

In many legends the yew is a symbol of ill-fated lovers who are truly united only in death - like Iseult, a lady of Ireland who was wedded to Mark, King of Cornwall, whom she did not love. Iseult's mother prepared a love potion to make her daughter fall in love with her new husband, but it was drunk instead by Mark's nephew, Tristan. He and Iseult fell passionately in love and, after many partings and tricks of fate, they died in each other's arms. Tristan and Iseult are said to have been buried above Merlin's Cave at Tintagel Castle in Cornwall, England, where, within a year, a yew tree sprouted from each grave. Three times King Mark cut the yew trees down and three times they grew back, until finally Mark gave in and allowed them to grow. At last their branches reached toward each other, becoming so entwined that they could nevermore be parted.

LESSON OF THE YEW

As a tree whose possible life outspans that of all other trees as well as much of the course of human history to date, the yew is symbolic of the sum of all wisdom. Just as the yew contains the lessons of all the other trees, so, it is said, do we contain all the experiences, knowledge, and understanding of our ancestors. The yew tree reminds us of this possibility. It emphasizes the relatively brief span of a human life and the short-term nature of many of our beliefs and practices, which so often prove inadequate over time. As the culmination of the spiritual journey, the ultimate lesson of the yew is the transcendence of death.

HEALING

The flesh of the *red fruits* is harmless, but the *seeds* themselves are toxic. The poisons are absorbed by the body within minutes. In small amounts they slow the heartbeat and cause collapse and gastroenteritis; in larger doses they can cause sudden death. Yew was once used to treat snake bites and rabies. An alkaloid named taxol has recently been discovered in yew needles that seems to be effective against ovarian cancer, and laboratories and drug companies now buy *yew clippings* in bulk for their research. In homeopathic medicine, tinctures made from yew are used to treat cystitis, headaches, neuralgia, dimness of vision, infections of the heart, liver, kidneys, and urinary tract, as well as gout, rheumatism, and arthritis.

Greenman Essence of Yew aids memory and discrimination, helps the immune system, and increases energy. It is said to protect from harm by activating the highest spiritual values of survival and protection.

CAUTION

ALL PARTS OF THE YEW ARE EXTREMELY POISONOUS. YEW SHOULD THEREFORE NEVER BE COLLECTED FOR SELF-MEDICATION OR ADMINISTERED TO OTHERS.

Colors Black, Dark Green *Planet* Saturn

Stone Olivine *Polarity* Feminine

Metal Lead *Element* Earth

Deities Banbha, Hecate

Resurrection

Death + Rebirth

Eternity

Access to the Ancestors + the Spirit Realms

Nameless Day

Appeasing the Dark Queen...

ONE DAY REMAINS completely unaccounted for in the Celtic Calendar, December 22nd, known as the "Nameless Day." This is the extra day that features in so many folk tales where the story takes place over a year and a day. On this day, when the King of the Waning Year was dead and the new King of the Waxing Year not yet born, it was the custom to fast to appease the goddess in her darkest aspect so that she would permit the sun to return to the world and the cycle of the year to recommence. This darkest of days has neither tree nor name and is sacred to the Morrigan, goddess of death and destruction. Her name means Great Queen in Irish. She appears in Arthurian legend as Morgan le Faye, sister of King Arthur: "le Faye" means "the Fate." This dark queen took the form of a raven and was feared and respected by everyone.

On this day it was the custom to fast to appease the Dark Queen, so that she would allow the sun to return to the world.

Pine *Tree of Nativity*

DECEMBER 23RD
Birthday of the Divine Child

Pinus sylvestris
SCOT'S PINE

Pinus strobus
EASTERN WHITE PINE
— "THE PINE THAT
BUILT AMERICA"

Birth of the King of the Waxing Year...

APPROXIMATELY 120 SPECIES of pine are found throughout the northern hemisphere, from the Arctic Circle to as far south as North Africa and Southeast Asia. The one with which the Irish and Scots Celts would have been most familiar is the Scot's Pine. Its lifespan can be as long as 600 years, although generally it is around 250 years. Height depends on soil: in good conditions it reaches 120 feet or more. Scot's Pine needles are two to three inches long and produced in pairs. They are flexible with a waxy coating that prevents water loss and gives the foliage a bluish sheen. The White Pine carries its needles in groups of five.

Male and female flowers are produced on the same tree. In dry weather, the small yellow male flowers release clouds of sulfur-yellow pollen. Female flowers are tiny red cone-like buds held at the tip of each new spring shoot to catch the pollen and draw it into their sticky ovules. It takes two to three summers for cones to fully develop. Then, when the weather is sufficiently dry and warm, they open to reveal small brown winged seeds, which are carried off by the wind or eaten and distributed by birds. It is possible to find three generations of cone on a single branch – the current year's newly formed cones at the tip, then the previous year's fertilized cones with their seeds still tightly sealed inside and, further still up the branch, older cones that have already shed their seeds to the wind. Scot's Pine bark is reddish and divided into scaly plates in mature trees. The bark on the upper part of the tree is smoother and much redder, especially when wet.

Pine resin was made into sealing wax and used to line beer barrels and seal boats, and to wax violin bows. Pine pitch – oil or tar of pine – was used as an antiseptic as well as a preservative and sealant. Turpentine is a product of pine resin and pine sap makes a potent wine. The tall timber is used especially for ships' masts, pit props, telephone poles, and railway sleepers.

Pine forests the world over have always been plundered in times of war. The ancient remains of Scotland's native pine forests were devastated during the First and Second World Wars, largely for making ammunition boxes. Timber from northern pine forests, known as deal, is best used in the construction industry as it is much harder than wood from southern pines.

The Scot's Pine can live as long as 600 years and grows up to 200 feet or more.

MYSTICAL ASSOCIATIONS

The pine is a feminine tree, as are all the trees of the five vowels in the ogham alphabet, five being the sacred number of the White Goddess. The first of the vowels is pine, the birth tree. In ancient Greece the pine was sacred to Artemis, the moon goddess who presided over childbirth, and the pine still remains the prime birth tree in Northern Europe today. The Norway spruce (which is a kind of pine) is the familiar tree of Christ's nativity, whose birth is now celebrated on December 25th, rather than the older traditional date of December 23rd. This day anciently marked the dawn of the light half of the year and the birthday of the Divine Child, the new King of the Waxing Year.

In Europe, Druids burned huge fires of pine and yew at the Winter Solstice to draw back the sun god from the Underworld so that he could be reborn into this world. Druantia, a Gallic fir goddess also known as Queen of the Druids, was celebrated at this time. These great fires of the Winter Solstice later became the custom of burning the Yule log. Pines were decorated with lights and shiny objects during Yuletide to preserve the divine light, the sacred life-giving light of the sun god, which is traditionally carried through the dark days of winter by all evergreen plants. Later the Christmas tree carried on this tradition in celebration of Christ, whose birth was announced by the appearance of a new star in the sky, and in whose

The pine is the totem tree of the goddess Druantia, who is also known as Queen of the Druids.

memory a star is placed at the top of the tree. In the Word Ogham of Aonghus, Ailm is given as the beginning of answers. In the Word Ogham of Morainn it is the loudest of groans, whether pleasure or pain, such as the sounds of love-making and of childbirth.

The pine is also closely connected with all gods of wine like Dionysus and Bacchus. In Greek legend, Dionysus gave the mortal Icarius the knowledge of making wine from grapes. Icarius tried out his first draught on some shepherds, who became drunk and, thinking they were bewitched, murdered Icarius and buried him beneath a pine tree. When she heard of her father's murder, Icarius' daughter Erigone, stricken with grief, hanged herself from a pine. All over ancient Athens sympathetic maidens were found hanging dead from pines. This continued until Icarus' murder was avenged.

The pine cone is a phallic symbol of the gods' fecundity. Ariadne, the orgiastic goddess, whose worship often demanded blood sacrifice, was represented at the Dionysian revels by an ivy-entwined, fir-cone-tipped branch. Her devotees, the Bacchae, drank pine-sap wine, laced with ivy and fly agaric, which caused them in their ravings to tear to pieces all who crossed their path. Greek legend also tells how the pine became evergreen. Rhea (goddess of the new moon and wife of Cronos) was betrayed by her lover Atys, so she avenged herself by turning Atys into a pine tree. Then, filled with remorse, she wept beneath the tree, where Zeus took pity on her and decreed that the tree would ever more keep its leaves so that the young goddess could enjoy their company the year round.

Because pine cones grow spirally on the branches, they were thought to be good conductors of magical energy, their clock-wise pattern following the earth's movement around the sun. Pine cones were used in fertility rites and pine pollen was used in money spells because its color was believed to attract gold. Hanging pine branches over doors and windows is traditionally believed to prevent evil entering a building, and carrying a pine cone is believed to impart vigor to the old. Pine resin is burned to clear negative energies, being said to repel evil and

return negative energy to its source. This can also be done by scattering pine needles around. North American Indians put bags of pine needles under the heads of those who cannot sleep. Doctors to the pharaohs of ancient Egypt used pitch and turpentine to treat pneumonia, and the oil distilled from pine resin remains a tried-and-tested remedy for colds and bronchial complaints around the world today.

LESSON OF THE PINE

From its lofty position above the tops of most other trees, the pine reminded ancient peoples of the importance of taking the overview, encouraging objectivity and farsightedness. We are advised to cleanse ourselves of negativity, neither dwelling on mistakes nor apportioning blame. Fir is a symbol of the elevated mind and the birth of the spiritual warrior.

The pine remains the prime birth tree in Northern Europe and North America today. It is, of course, the Christmas Tree.

❦ HEALING ❦

An infusion of *pine needles* makes an effective inhalant to relieve congestion and irritation of the mucus membranes. It is antiseptic, expectorant, and tonic. Pine-needle tea or tea made from fresh *pine shoots* aids the healing of bladder and kidney problems, and infections of the urinary tract. A decoction of the young spring *buds* will also ease cystitis and rheumatism, as well as bronchial complaints. Modern science has shown that pine *needles and shoots* are especially rich in Vitamin A and C and pine tea is a traditional and effective cure for scurvy. A decoction of the *cones and needles* used in the bath will ease breathing disorders, skin complaints, and rheumatic pain. The *essential oil* is used in aromatherapy for its antiseptic, antiviral, bactericidal, deodorant, and diuretic properties. In vibrational medicine, the Pine *Bach Flower Remedy* is useful for those who have a guilt complex, are self-reproachful, and who can never be satisfied with their achievements. The *Greenman Essence of Pine* brings insight, helping to activate the third eye and broaden perspective.

❦

Planets Mars, The Sun

Polarity Feminine *Metal* Gold

Deities Artemis, Ariadne, Rhea, Cybele, Durantia, Erigone, Dionysus, Bacchus

Foresight + Farsight

Purification

Objectivity

Birth

Beech *Tree of Learning*

THE WHOLE YEAR ROUND

National emblem of Denmark

Fagus sylvatica
COMMON BEECH

*Fagus sylvatica
'Purpurea'*
COPPER BEECH

Fagus grandifoila
AMERICAN BEECH

Sign of prosperity...

THERE ARE TEN species of beech widely distributed throughout the northern hemisphere. The Common Beech is a tall, elegant tree with feminine contours. The curves of its trunk and branches so much resemble parts of the human body that beech trees often appear like dryads (tree spirits) diving into or emerging from the earth. Their smooth, silvery-gray bark invites the touch and is a favorite with lovers, who often carve their affections into the tree's trunk.

Beeches are popular as ornamental trees in hilltop groves and avenues. They also make a good hedge. The beech favors chalky soil and is shallow-rooted, the roots often appearing above the ground. Because of this habit, the beech is prone to wind damage and is often completely uprooted in severe storms. Beech trees growing in the open tend to branch out low, while those in a woodland setting branch out higher, emphasizing their tall, sensuous trunks. Beech woods' lofty interiors are often compared to the inside of a cathedral. In spring, they are light and airy and often carpeted with a mass of bluebells. In contrast, the summer canopy lets through relatively little light and rain, discouraging dense undergrowth.

Beech leaves unfold fanlike in spring, when they are soft and a translucent golden-green. They harden and grow a darker green as the year progresses, turning through yellow to copper and gold in fall. The young leaves of the copper beech open pink, aging to purple-brown.

Male and female flowers are produced on the same tree, appearing about a month after the leaves. Female flowers develop a bristly brown outer husk that splits open when ripe, folding back to reveal two three-sided seeds. Oil from the seeds is used for cooking and lighting. In America it is called beechnut butter. The nuts, known as beechmast, are poisonous to horses but are a favorite food of squirrels, deer, cattle, pigs, and pheasants. When peeled and roasted, the nuts have also been used as a coffee substitute. The leaves were even given to German soldiers during the First World War in place of tobacco. Beech timber is fine-grained, knot-free, and pinkish-yellow with darker flecks. It bends easily and is especially good for making chairs and simple furniture, as well as tool handles and small implements, particularly spoons and spatulas.

Beech woods' lofty interiors are often compared to the inside of a cathedral.

MYSTICAL ASSOCIATIONS

Beech wood was once used to make writing tablets and thin slices bound together are said to have made the first ever book.

The beech tree is a symbol for the written word and for the innate wisdom contained within it, and for ancient learning. Thus the beech is symbolic of the sum of the wisdom of all the other trees. Beech was once used to make writing tablets and thin slices of beech wood bound together made the first book, previously scrolls had been used. This connection is evident in many of the languages of modern Europe. The Anglo-Saxon word for beech is *boc*, which later became book. The German for beech is *Buche*, which became *Buch* for book, and *Buchstabe* is the modern German word for letter, as in letter of the alphabet. The modern Swedish word *bok* means both book and beech tree.

The beech tree is associated with all gods of wisdom, learning, and the human intellect, including Ogma, the great warrior figure of the Tuatha De Danaan, who was deified as the early Celtic god Ogma Sunface, and who is said to have invented the ogham alphabet; the Greek god Hermes, the messenger; Thoth of the ancient Egyptians, god of wisdom and mathematics; Mercury, the Roman equivalent of Hermes; and Odin, supreme god of the Nordic tribes, who was given the gift of the runes. This was an equivalent to the ogham alphabet that, like ogham, is also used for esoteric communication and divination. As the tree of ancient learning, the beech is also associated with Cronos, Greek god of time and the cycle of the ages of man.

The wood and leaves of the beech tree are carried as a talisman to increase creative powers. Carving the words of a wish into a beech stick is said to make a wish come true – if it is meant to be. It is also said that if you bury a beech stick in the ground, the wish

The beech is the tree of learning and the written word, as well as a symbol of prosperity.

will be manifested as the wood decays and is reabsorbed by the earth. The beech's connections with the gods Odin and Ogma and the invention of mystical cypher alphabets also make the tree a symbol of divination. The beech is the national emblem of Denmark and a sign of prosperity.

The beech tree features in this excerpt from the ancient Welsh poem *Câd Goddeu,*

> *When the beech prospers,*
> *Though spells and litanies*
> *The oak tops entangle,*
> *There is hope for trees*
>
> "THE BARD," TALIESIN

the "Battle of the Trees," which is attributed to the 6th-century bard and magician Taliesin, and interpreted here by the poet Robert Graves:

> The tops of the beech tree
> Have sprouted of late,
> Are changed and renewed
> From their withered state.
>
> When the beech prospers,
> Though spells and litanies
> The oak tops entangle,
> There is hope for trees.

Although there will always be those who seek to manipulate and control others by restricting access to information and learning, and by slanting information available to suit their own ends, as long as the wisdom of the trees, which is the sum of all human knowledge and experience, is enshrined in writing, so there is hope.

LESSON OF THE BEECH

Year in and year out, the beech tree reminds us of the importance of learning and of the need to preserve our knowledge in writing for the benefit of generations to come. Just as lovers carve their names into the trunk of the beech so their love will grow with the tree, so must we continue to record our wisdom and understanding for future benefit. Rooted in the knowledge of the ancients and sustained by the ideas of the present, we will continue to reach for the stars.

The beech tree reminded our ancient ancestors of the need to preserve all knowledge in writing for the benefit of generations to come.

HEALING

The beech has few uses in conventional medicine, being most useful in the field of vibrational healing. *Beech tar* is an old remedy for skin disorders like eczema and psoriasis and mattresses stuffed with beech *leaves* were once thought to aid the healing process. Culpeper recommended the bruised leaves for reducing swellings and a poultice made from the leaves for healing scabs. *Water* collected at dawn from pools in the hollows of ancient beeches was believed to have great healing potential, especially for skin complaints.

Greenman Essence of Beech is recommended for those who need to boost their confidence and hope. It aids relaxation and the release of held-in trauma, improving confidence in self-expression, and promoting an easy-going attitude. The *Beech Bach Flower Remedy* helps promote tolerance. It is useful for those who find it hard to make allowances for the shortcomings of others and who are overcritical and lacking in sympathy. It helps us to see the good in all things.

Planets Mercury, Saturn

Polarity Feminine

Elements Air, Earth

Deities Ogma Sunface, Thoth, Hermes, Mercury, Odin, Cronos

Learning + Knowledge

Wisdom + Understanding

Prosperity

Index

ACKNOWLEDGEMENTS

Respectful thanks to the late Robert Graves for his translation of the ancient Welsh poem *Câd Goddeu*, "The Battle of the Trees." Great respect also to the Bard Taliesin to whom the poem is attributed and whose poetry was the inspiration behind this book. To all friends and family, thank you for your encouragement and practical help, especially to my mother and to her mother too. Thanks to Simon and Sue Lily at Greenman Tree Essences and to Jacqueline Memory Patterson for her insights into Druidic law. Big thanks to Redcliffe Professional Colour Laboratories in Bristol for their constant reliability, to Bridgewater Books for their consideration, and to David and Charles for their faith in the project. After a lifetime of interest and more than seven years of research and photography there are so many people to whom I am grateful for inspiration, knowledge, and assistance. Thank you for helping to carry the spirit behind the ancient Wisdom of Trees into a new millenium.

Jane Gifford
DECEMBER 1999

FOR MY MOTHER